The Golden Cord

The Golden Cord

*St. John Chrysostom's Vision
for the Family Revisited*

KRISTIN A. VARGAS

WIPF & STOCK · Eugene, Oregon

THE GOLDEN CORD
St. John Chrysostom's Vision for the Family Revisited

Copyright © 2022 Kristin A. Vargas. All rights reserved. Except for brief quotations in critical publications or reviews, no part of this book may be reproduced in any manner without prior written permission from the publisher. Write: Permissions, Wipf and Stock Publishers, 199 W. 8th Ave., Suite 3, Eugene, OR 97401.

Wipf & Stock
An Imprint of Wipf and Stock Publishers
199 W. 8th Ave., Suite 3
Eugene, OR 97401

www.wipfandstock.com

PAPERBACK ISBN: 978-1-6667-3316-7
HARDCOVER ISBN: 978-1-6667-2754-8
EBOOK ISBN: 978-1-6667-2755-5

03/08/22

Unless otherwise noted, Scripture quotations are from the ESV® Bible (The Holy Bible, English Standard Version®), copyright ©2001 by Crossway, a publishing ministry of Good News Publishers. Used by permission. All rights reserved.

Scripture quotations marked NKJV are from the New King James Version®, copyright ©1982 by Thomas Nelson. Used by permission. All rights reserved.

Scripture quotations marked NASB are from the New American Standard Bible®, copyright ©2020 by The Lockman Foundation. Used by permission. All rights reserved. www.lockman.org.

Scripture quotations marked GNT are from the Good News Translation in Today's English Version, second edition, copyright ©1992 by American Bible Society. Used by permission.

Scripture quotations marked GW are from *GOD'S WORD*®, copyright ©1995 by God's Word to the Nations Mission Society. Used by permission.

Scripture quotations marked NLT are from the Holy Bible, New Living Translation, copyright ©1996, 2004, 2015 by Tyndale House Foundation. Used by permission of Tyndale House Publishers, Carol Stream, Illinois 60188. All rights reserved.

Scripture quotations marked NIV are from the Holy Bible, New International Version®, copyright ©1973, 1978, 1984, 2011 by Biblica, Inc®. Used by permission of Zondervan. All rights reserved worldwide.

To my "little church": Hugo, Ethan, Judith, and Margaret.

Whatever He commanded our fathers
To make these things known to their children,
That a different generation may know,
Children yet to be born;
And they will arise, and declare these
Things to their children,
So they may put their hope in God . . .

—Ps 77:5–7

What Jesus invites us to imitate is his own *desire*, the spirit that directs him toward the goal on which his intention is fixed: to resemble God the Father as much as possible.

—René Girard

Our salvation is in treasures wherein is wisdom, knowledge, and godliness toward the Lord—these are the treasures of righteousness.

—Isa 33:6, St. Athanasius Academy Septuagint

Contents

Acknowledgments — ix

1. We Live in a Moral Dystopia — 1
2. St. John Chrysostom and the "Little Church" — 23
3. Becoming Real: *Askesis* and Spiritual Formation — 50
4. East of Eden: Imitation and Fatherhood — 79
5. Story-Telling: Threads of the Cord — 108

Conclusion: The Golden Cord — 143

Bibliography — 149

Subject Index — 155

Acknowledgments

I FIRST THANK MY husband, Hugo, for his steadfast support throughout the writing of this book. He never fails to encourage and motivate me in whatever I seek to accomplish. I am grateful to all those past and present professors and mentors who have guided my curiosity and research. I especially thank Dr. Charles K. Bellinger, who introduced me to a whole new world of thought; archivist Jill Botticelli and historian Terry Christian for their moral support and friendship; Dr. Evan Lenow, who made me read so many invaluable primary sources; Dr. William Goff for his wisdom and guidance; Dr. Stephen Presley for his insight concerning patristic Christianity and for steering me through the dissertation process; and Fr. Mark McNary of St. Peter Orthodox Church for being my spiritual guide through my conversion to Orthodoxy, which occurred during the process of writing this book. Last but not least, I thank my mother, Judy, for all the time she spent watching my toddlers when I needed to write.

1

We Live in a Moral Dystopia

IN 2016, I BECAME a mother. Motherhood changed the direction of my life in a way I had not anticipated. Up to that point, I had pursued my interest in history and theology, hoping someday to teach Christian history in higher education. Little did I suspect at that point that my pursuit of knowledge would veer into the arena of ethics. Yet by the time I was pregnant again, only a year and a half later, I was halfway through a doctoral program in ethics with my eye on quite a different subject to research and teach.

During this time, I discovered radio personality Dennis Prager, who has a weekly Ultimate Issues Hour. Sometimes he brings up the subject of parenthood, and when this happens, he often tells parents to spend their time focusing on what they consider to be the most important thing to instill in their children. He cautions his listeners that kids will tune out their parent if pulled in too many directions. Thus, he recommends picking the one thing the parent is concerned about most, whether that be good grades, sports, the arts, etc. He notes that teaching goodness is not the top concern, perhaps seen as a byproduct of overall good parenting or education. However, he believes wise parents intentionally make goodness the "one thing" they focus on above all else.

I think Dennis Prager is right on this, and I thought as much back in 2016 with the birth of my son. Yet the question of *how* to raise a good person was a mystery. The question is one of moral formation, and so I found myself abandoning my original trajectory of history and moving into ethics. One of the most important books I read during this transition into my study of morality was Alasdair MacIntyre's *After Virtue*.

For those not familiar with the book, let me give a short introduction. The first several pages of *After Virtue* describe a hypothetical apocalypse followed by a dystopian world where all that is left of scientific knowledge are the barest fragments of notes, textbooks, and journals.[1] Post-apocalyptic explorers dig through the ashes of laboratories and elementary schools, hoping to find bits and pieces of an ancient and forgotten discipline. Gathering remnants of pages from books and notes, these new "scientists" cobble together what they believe is the lost knowledge of the past. Yet how can they know that their new interpretation is nonsense or if their methodologies are even fruitful? What is now called "science" is conducted wholly without its original context and has little resemblance to actual science as practiced before the apocalypse. So not only are the theories developed wrongly, but also the process used to arrive at those conclusions is absent the foundation of fundamental principles. MacIntyre then applies this hypothetical situation to Western civilization in the case of morality. He proposes that Westerners are living within a morally contextless and ambiguous society, which has led to the unspoken consensus of *emotivism* as the default moral position. Emotivism is the view that moral judgments are not based in reality but are instead simply expressions of feelings or preferences.

MacIntyre is positioned within one stream of moral thought that he calls the morality of tradition. The concept of tradition as moral authority found its "apocalypse" during the Enlightenment project, whose thinkers developed other moral options that rose to prominence. There are at least six intellectual streams that diverged from the fountain of the Enlightenment, which represent alternate views and choices on how to think morally. It is these alternative streams of thought that make up the failed Enlightenment project, according to MacIntyre and other cultural critics, and that obliterated the last remains of a world where moral concepts made sense.

If MacIntyre's argument is correct, then most people do not have a coherent, explicit moral position. If they claim to, they underestimate the implicit moral positions they have absorbed from culture. This means most of us muddle around with opposing and paradoxical beliefs. How could this not be so, if one considers the impact of popular psychology, or popular political ideology, and so on.

In contrast to the present confusing and incoherent modern moral context, I had to stop and consider the nature of morality, what it is, and

---

1. See MacIntyre, *After Virtue*, 1.

how it is formed. Like other capabilities, morality is developed, learned, and nurtured in human beings who have the inborn capacity for making ethical judgments. Moral education starts at a young age. Given MacIntyre's theory, where does the Christian ethic fit in this contextless, moral dystopia, especially regarding the moral development of the young? How do Christian parents like myself, I wondered, intentionally guide and cultivate the Christian moral life as described in Scripture and the Christian tradition in a society that is so morally mixed up? The young cannot learn without good teachers, and the first teachers a child encounters are his or her parents. Yet parents cannot teach what they do not know, much less practice. The central focus of my quest became an attempt to answer these questions concerning the moral formation of the Christian family as a symbiotic whole and its place within the church, set within the morally gray lands of Western society and without the benefit of a tradition rejected and destroyed by the Enlightenment.

SO WHAT?

Given the moral conditions presented by Alasdair MacIntyre, the main question I pursue is this: how should the Christian family undertake moral formation? Parents and educators alike might be tempted to offer a variety of answers. These answers are derived from a mishmash of quasi-moralistic responses taken from the *zeitgeist* of the times, philosophical and therapeutic ideologies smuggled in as "common sense." I know firsthand that Christians are not immune to the pressure of cultural forces that have been shaped from blatantly anti-Christian worldviews. Saint John Chrysostom, the ancient teacher who became the focus of my studies, did not underestimate the importance of this problem. Likewise, Chrysostom's congregation in Antioch of Syria was not immune to the societal pressure of the pagan philosophical and religious institutions that had reigned in their not-so-distant past. History rhymes, if not repeats, and each era, the fourth century and the twenty-first, has produced a wealth of philosophies and belief systems for Christians to battle. This struggle is not easy, as the influence of these systems infuses the air everyone, the Christian and the agnostic, the religious and the atheist, breathes.

Chrysostom believed that Christian character formation, especially within the family, acted as a lifeline through treacherous cultural waters. He uses the metaphor of a golden cord, or chain, to describe his system of education, each link in the chain as a Christian family raising morally upright children, who then grow up to become the next link, raising up the next generation this way, and the next in a continuous line.

Chrysostom and his "golden cord" present Christians with another option from the vast resources of the premodern era. The incredible treasury of collective wisdom on the Christian life, the fruit borne out of the first millennia is largely ignored, or more likely, long forgotten in the average Christian circle. Still, this heritage is available to all Christians and, with it, the knowledge of spiritual formation in the life of Christ.

The Christian ethic relied upon by Chrysostom and many of his contemporaries is *theanthropic*. The theanthropic ethic is Trinitarian and incarnational, built upon the dual work of Christ and the Holy Spirit. It is not only a virtue ethic, for the Christian also embodies Christ's fulfillment of the law, as well as Christian freedom. In its fullness, this Christian *ethos* is teleological and perfectionistic, deontological and virtue-based, situational and existential, interpersonal and evangelical. This ethic cannot be pigeonholed into one of these categories, because it is not systematic and includes all of these elements. The aim of the theanthropic ethic is transfiguration: the transformation from the old human to the new. Stanley Harakas gives this characterization: "In the deepest, most existential sense, human nature is 'theanthroponomous,' that is, in order to become fully human, we must become God-like."[2] The theanthropic ethic is missing in the contemporary culture and desperately needs to be rediscovered, so that the Christian family can guard against the simulacra of morality that is so invasive in our modern context.

I argue for the return to the theanthropic ethic of the premodern church. The Christian family can adopt this ethic, accept Chrysostom's view of family as a "little church," and use his pedagogy—broadened and reconceptualized for contemporary culture—as a guide for moral formation. The Christian family is meant to undergo *askesis* together, which enables the taming of the passions, the cultivation of Christian character, and the drawing nearer to God.[3]

WHY ST. JOHN CHRYSOSTOM?

Since the question I have asked as a parent—how to raise godly children—concerns revisiting a premodern ethic, another question must be answered: why John Chrysostom? After all, the theanthropic ethic is drawn from multiple sources, including the early fathers of Christianity: Athanasius, Basil of Caesarea, Gregory of Nyssa, Maximus the Confessor, and others. Indeed,

---

2. Harakas, *Toward Transfigured Life*, 21–22.

3. *Askesis* means practicing spiritual exercises that include (but are not limited to) prayer, fasting, and almsgiving. It can also be understood as spiritual warfare.

these voices of the past are relied upon in the following chapters to situate the contemporary parent within the premodern theology-ethic drawn upon. Chrysostom fits this project in several significant ways, which is why he remains the model and the key witness for a reintroduction of moral education similar to what MacIntyre proposes as a morality of tradition.

The primary reason to turn to Chrysostom resides in the pastoral nature of his work. He is not a first-tier thinker in the sense of the great theologians of his time (e.g., Basil of Caesarea). Instead, he is remembered for being a great orator and teacher. His interpretation of the Sermon on the Mount, for example, was adopted as official church doctrine by both Eastern and Western Catholicism (the latter lasting into the Middle Ages). He concentrated most of his efforts on the daily problems and issues that arise in pastoral care. Therefore, behind Chrysostom's practical counsel and preaching, the following chapters borrow from first-tier thinkers for the deeper theological and ethical moorings upon which his spirituality rested. His writings are practical, and ethics is nothing if not practical. He is most concerned with the Christian life of his people, and he cares about the same concerns that they did. He is sympathetic to the needs of parents and children, especially those in a pluralistic, affluent society.

The second reason is the corpus of his work is vast. As a pastor first and foremost, he is highly concerned with the problems that plagued his well-to-do congregation in Antioch. He spends most of his time preaching on wealth and poverty, marriage and family. Even if he had never written his treatise on the latter, the same concepts can be found in his homilies.

Another key point is the extensive access to his work. Eight hundred of his sermons are still available today, and the fact that he is so readable, sixteen hundred years later, is a testament to the relevancy of his writings through centuries.[4] It is a simple fact that he survived the ages.

THE APPROACH

In this book, I seek to revisit an early interpretation of Christian theology, ethics, and spiritual formation in order to present a contemporary model of Christian education that critiques post-Enlightenment thought. In other words, this is my attempt to offer Christians another option for moral education that combats the secular humanist approach that dominates current culture.

Throughout this book, I rely on the Eastern theology of the first one thousand years of Christianity. I believe building the foundation from the

---

4. Volz, "Genius of Chrysostom's Preaching."

Greek perspective will allow for the transcendence of the diverse strands of Christian tradition and present a holistic vision of Christian character formation. If the hermeneutic relied solely on contemporary theology, then it would continue to be informed by the scholastic tradition and post-Enlightenment understanding of theology and ethics. Instead, the theanthropic ethic recovers a premodern way of understanding the relationship between theology and ethics.

The second reason for this exploratory effort is to strip away preconceptions by relying on a tradition that is outside of the norm. Receiving this epoch's wisdom through the interpretive lens of a tradition that is not using a hermeneutic of suspicion, one that sees innate worth in the work of desert ascetics and early fathers, will be an antidote to the skepticism of post-Enlightenment theology. That being said, the Christian vantage point I take is unapologetically that of the Eastern (Greek) Christian tradition. There are notable exceptions. I borrow from two voices outside of the theological discipline to give this work a multifaceted understanding of human nature and the moral life: anthropological philosopher René Girard and moral philosopher Alasdair MacIntyre. These two thinkers inform the theological anthropology that is presented in the following chapters.

The third reason for my use of a premodern bias is to avoid the fall into a "re-enactment of the old Christological struggle," the propensity to overemphasize human psychology at the expense of the incarnation (Nestorianism) or to reduce the human being's ability to cooperate with the Holy Spirit in any meaningful way (monophysitism).[5] These two errors in theology are seen today by other names in contemporary parlance, namely liberal theology and neoorthodoxy.

I have a two-part trajectory: to extend MacIntyre's thesis in *After Virtue* and to resource a premodern thinker for contemporary ethics. The double aim will push the envelope of how parents understand tradition, moral formation, and the Christian life. Overall, my approach marries Girard's groundbreaking mimetic theory and MacIntyre's concept of the "narratable life" to ancient Christian spirituality as received through Chrysostom.

THE AIM OF THIS BOOK

My goal is to give Christian parents and Christian educators alike a deeper understanding of the cultural moral climate in which children are being

---

5. Florovsky, *Bible, Church, Tradition*, 6. This phrase describes the tendencies to overemphasize humanity's ability and role (Nestoriansim) or underemphasize it (monophysitism) that are repeated in history time and time again.

raised and of the ancient Christian wisdom tradition that has the power to counteract this environment. Chrysostom's system of education complements a classical education (indeed, this type of education was what he was raised in and most familiar with) but can still be implemented, to an extent, without this kind of setting. After they read this book, it is my hope that Christian parents and educators should better know the cultural forces they face in raising Christian children. The idea is to orient the reader within the Christian tradition with another option on how to move forward with the moral growth of their families and students.

On a more general level, I wrote this book for anyone who desires to rethink distinctions between spirituality and ethics, moral growth and virtue. The borrowing of Girard's thought in conjunction with Eastern Christian theology contributes to scholarly research. The hermeneutic used grants various traditions new insight into spiritual formation and the Christian life. At the very least, this book should add to ecumenical and interfaith dialogue.

THE CURRENT CULTURAL MORALITY

There are at least six streams of thought that flow through the current cultural landscape—emotivism, subjectivism, Nietzschean existentialism, liberal theology, the therapeutic movement, and modern gnosticism—that compete with the theanthropic ethic and disagree on key points.[6] The commonality of these opposing belief systems is that they are all post-Enlightenment. This is where the argument for a return to an ancient wisdom tradition focuses its critique. In order to understand why it behooves the Christian parent to practice an ancient form of Christian moral and spiritual formation, he or she needs to know the opposing, anti-Christian spirits (ethics) against which they are guarding their families. Not only are Christians told by the apostles to arm themselves against the lies of the principalities and powers, but ancient prophetic voices from the Hebrew Bible use the language of the guard, insisting that the righteous be vigilant watchmen. Jesus Christ echoes those, like Ezekiel, who use this language, especially in his parables. Part of being watchmen and watchwomen for Christ is to know what the thieves and wolves look like.

---

6. This list is not exhaustive and is based on the conclusions of a variety of scholars and cultural critics, including MacIntyre, *After Virtue*; Bellinger, *Trinitarian Self*; Rieff, *Triumph of the Therapeutic*; Delsol, *Unlearned Lessons*; Girard, *I See Satan Fall*.

Emotivism and Subjectivism

The first contextual problem zones confronted by Christian parents are in the two metaethical categories of emotivism and subjectivism. As I mentioned before, the first is well known thanks to its treatment in *After Virtue*. MacIntyre's definition of emotivism is useful: "Emotivism is the doctrine that all evaluative judgments and more specifically moral judgments are *nothing but* expressions of preference, expressions of attitude or feeling, insofar as they are moral or evaluative in character."[7] In other words, there are no universal moral values, just opinions.

David Hume is a good example of an emotivist, as his work continues to be widely read and is influential in many disciplines, including ethics. Following his teacher, Francis Hutcheson, Hume rejected rational ethics. In his *Treatise of Human Nature*, he writes, "Reason is, and ought only to be the slave of the passions, and can never pretend to any other office than to serve and obey them."[8] He does not believe reason, or moral judgments based on reason, is enough to motivate an individual to act. Morality lies in *feelings*. "Morality, therefore, is more properly felt than judged of . . . . To have the sense of virtue is nothing but to *feel* a satisfaction of a particular kind from the contemplation of a character. The very feeling constitutes our praise or admiration."[9]

In *An Enquiry Concerning the Principles of Morals*, Hume has more to say concerning the source of sentiments, and attributes the development of moral distinctions and rules to universal sentiments of "censure or approbation," while virtues arise from feelings of praise and pleasure.[10] Hume regards moral language and law as the human invention that restrains universally repugnant acts or encourages universally pleasant behaviors.

The second theory that is prevalent in our culture is subjectivism. Subjectivism is part of the cognitivist branch of the metaethics taxonomy, and both individual relativism and cultural relativism are within its scope. Unlike emotivism, subjectivism affirms the reality of values, albeit subjective to the individual or culture. An individual might have a principle he holds to be true but believes that it is not true for his neighbor. The same can be applied to cultures. Thus, meaning is subjective to the person or culture and not an objective truth that exists substantially beyond these realms.

---

7. MacIntyre, *After Virtue*, 11–12.
8. Hume, *Treatise of Human Nature*, 2.3.3.
9. Hume, *Treatise of Human Nature*, 3.1–2.
10. Hume, *Enquiry Concerning Principles*, 10.1.

An example of an influential relativist is Joseph Fletcher. Although Fletcher considered himself a casuist (or neo-casuistic), the nature of his ethical method makes Fletcher an intellectual champion for subjectivism. He views morality as confined strictly to the situation at hand, relative to the individual making the moral decision. He effectually makes the situation primary in the making of moral decisions. He states, "Everything else without exception, all laws and rules and principles and ideals and norms, are only *contingent*, only valid *if they happen* to serve love in any situation."[11] The only goal he sees for the ethical person is to "serve love," but what Fletcher means by love is ambiguous, a "good feeling," and can be interpreted to mean anything to anybody.

Nietzschean Existentialism

The next alternative to MacIntyre's moral perspective lies within moral philosophy. Similar to subjectivism is philosophical existentialism. Existentialism arose as a reaction against Hegelian essentialism and is described as an attitude or mood, not a theory. Existentialism precedes essence or is the movement toward the self. One form of existentialism, which concerns me the most in our current culture, is rooted in Nietzschean thought. One of this type of existentialism's notable features is the rejection of systems and worldviews. For the existentialist, knowledge is found in the consciousness of the individual. This means that knowledge is subjective to the individual person, and truth is never objective. The key virtue for the existentialist is freedom: the absolute freedom of a person to determine his or her own path, decisions, and private beliefs. Therefore, the human being's purpose in life is to live authentically, and to *not* act on one's own terms is inauthentic, which is the only sin.

The atheistic existentialist does not believe in ultimate reality. Life is meaningless and absurd, and a person's interactions with other people are necessary only insofar as they help one become authentic. Other people are mainly viewed in the negative, however, because others *limit* freedom. Thus, others are a necessary evil: necessary to grow more authentic but evil if they prevent or limit the individual's choices or freedom.

While this philosophy sounds pessimistic, authenticity as a virtue is highly regarded in the current culture, as is freedom of choice. The cultural battle over abortion is a reminder of the power of this philosophy. In the current orthodoxy of the age, freedom of choice has gained status as a virtue that supersedes all other virtues that might hinder or narrow this freedom.

---

11. Fletcher, *Situation Ethics*, 30.

The rise of freedom of choice in the present hierarchy of virtues can be seen as far back as the nineteenth century. Consider the precursor to atheistic existentialism, Friedrich Nietzsche, who describes the "lord of the free will" who is freed from all moral restraints and able to seek empowerment through his own will. This concept is still attractive today. One can find this figure depicted in both current literature and film as either a rebellious, misunderstood hero or a sympathetic anti-hero. Existentialism in literature saw its heyday in the 1950s, but its undeniable impact on other disciplines (e.g., psychology and theology) means it continues to be a relevant current of intellectual discourse in the twenty-first century. Existentialist thinkers include Jean-Paul Sartre, Martin Heidegger, Rudolf Bultmann, and Nietzsche.

Liberal Theology and Schleiermacher

The next alternative to the theanthropic ethic concerns hermeneutics, which determines how meaning is understood, and the development of liberal theology by Friedrich Schleiermacher. Schleiermacher developed this "secular theory of interpretation" and viewed hermeneutics as an art form, specifically the art of understanding. This art can be applied to any form of writing, from sacred texts and literature to legal documents. Schleiermacher reacted to the rationalism of the Enlightenment by rejecting metaphysics and morals as the foundation of religious phenomena and instead viewed religion as experiential. Religion is not rational but deals with one's "living, acting, and feeling in relation to his creaturely dependence on God."[12]

Schleiermacher is considered the father of modern theology, and part of the reason for this is his use of novel idioms, such as "God-consciousness," which describes "the feeling of absolute dependence" on God.[13] Schleiermacher paved the way for nineteenth-century theological liberalism. His massive systematic theology, *Christian Faith*, anticipates schools of thought found in contemporary theology. His work influenced a great number of thinkers, including Wilhelm Dilthey and Rudolf Bultmann.

Schleiermacher also viewed hermeneutics as the art of understanding dialogue. This idea served as the basis for special hermeneutics, such as biblical interpretation. As his view of hermeneutics was picked up by disciplines outside of theology, it became adopted by secular culture.

Schleiermacher, like Hume and Fletcher, overemphasizes the single individual's self-consciousness and emotions above all other human capacities. All these thinkers sense that the Enlightenment experiment of reducing

12. R. Palmer, *Hermeneutics*, 85.
13. Schleiermacher, in Stroup, *Reformed Reader*, 113.

knowledge to the rational plane had failed and attempt to correct this mistake. This overemphasis and reaction are seen in the next moral alternative: psychology.

The Therapeutic Movement and its Prophets

Philip Rieff was a sociologist, not a psychologist, yet in his prescient book *The Triumph of the Therapeutic*, he predicted the rise of psychology and the "psychological person" replacing the religious person. Rieff foresaw the psychological quest for "self-actualization" usurping religion in the lives of westerners. One commentator, in an article that addresses Oprah Winfrey's success as the "prophet" of the therapeutic movement, explains, "In therapeutic culture, 'the self' becomes an individual's vocation, and authority becomes self-imposed, rather than handed down through religious or communal tradition."[14] This concept disregards the premodern view of the *telos*, or a natural end for the human being, a view upheld by Chrysostom.

An example of the psychologist-as-prophet is Richard Weissbourd, child and family psychologist and a faculty member at Harvard's School of Education. What he says about moral education and parental influence provides insight into the current topic. Weissbourd argues that emotions are "engines of moral learning." Positive emotions are important, but negative emotions like shame and fear are vitally necessary as well in shaping morality and behavior in society.[15] He asserts that painful feelings are important to moral development and that it is destructive for parents to protect their children from them. He further argues the current trend to erase negative emotions from the child's experience is problematic. The result of this censoring is a generation of young adults who cannot deal with shame and fear.

According to the moral psychology Weissbourd professes, parents have the primary role of either counteracting or generating emotions like shame in their children. When parents fail to teach manners, curb obnoxious characteristics, or rein in impulses, they set up their children for future relational problems. What is Weissbourd's remedy? A heavy dose of self-reflection in the parents themselves.

Note the emphasis on emotion. Weissbourd sees the parental role (in terms of moral development) as emotion cultivator and regulator. His remedy of self-reflection and moral growth on the part of the parent is to learn to sympathize with the child. This perspective seems close to Adam Smith's

---

14. Manson, "Oprah and the Triumph."
15. Weissbourd, *Parents We Mean to Be*, 10–11.

theory, which is akin to emotivism.[16] The parent is supposed to grow (as a self) in order to sympathize with the children enough to aid their emotional intelligence so that they, too, can develop into moral persons. Yet how the parent matures, apart from introspection, remains in question.

Weissbourd fits Rieff's concept of the psychologist as prophet. Rieff furthermore saw Freud and his heirs as fostering the "deconversion" experience of the West, and in doing so replacing religion as the primary source of morality, with psychotherapy "sanctioned mainly as a post-religious science of moral management."[17] This leads back to the self, unrestrained and "free" to become more authentic, to re-create humanity in its own image.

Modern Gnosticism

This overview of post-Enlightenment alternatives to the theanthropic ethic ends in the sphere of political-religious thought, specifically modern gnosticism. One of the great voices in this area is political philosopher Eric Voegelin. Voegelin redefined the antique term *gnosticism* to fit modernity.[18] He saw gnosticism as the belief that "it is possible to eliminate evil from the world and to establish a state of earthly bliss by, in effect, re-creating man."[19] In *The New Science of Politics*, he further describes gnosticism as the "fallacious immanentization of the Christian eschaton."[20] Voegelin viewed Nazism and Stalinism at their core as "religious phenomena."[21]

This kind of gnosticism, embodied in thinkers such as Nietzsche and Marx, is fundamentally anti-Christian. It is the reverse of the theanthropic ethic. It is the concept that "God is dead," the utopian ideal that humanity can make heaven on earth happen without the Creator. It is the religion of unbelief. As one commentator put it:

> The extent is enormous. Voegelin never provided a complete catalogue, but one may say that among the gnostic ideologies with which we are faced every day are: progressivism, positivism, egalitarianism, Freudianism, Marxist and non-Marxist

---

16. Adam Smith's concept of morality holds that the human moral sense is derived from the emotional capacity to sympathize with other people, whether directly or indirectly, and to seek praise and avoid blameworthy behavior (see Smith, *Theory of Moral Sentiments*).

17. Rieff, *Triumph of the Therapeutic*, 221.

18. Voegelin, *Modernity without Restraint*, 189.

19. Schram, "New Gnosticism."

20. Voegelin, *Modernity without Restraint*, 187.

21. Bellinger, *Genealogy of Violence*, 126.

socialism, scientism, that civil libertarianism which follows in the footsteps of John Stuart Mill's progressivism, that conservatism which seeks to 'freeze' history at a particular point in time, feminism, pacifism, and idealism (as opposed to realism) in international politics. Some of these ideologies emphasize movement toward a goal rather than the nature of the goal pursued, progressivism being the best example, but they are still gnostic.[22]

Gnosticism rejects reality. Its ancient form was notable for its demonization of the material realm. In our contemporary era, it also rejects tradition, specifically the wisdom tradition of all eras previous to this one. By this rejection, a new reality can be created, which is ordered by the human will. This is escapism, fleeing one world to a new, and it can be seen in the "modern thought forms" listed in the quote above.[23]

Against Post-Enlightenment Error

In following the trail of MacIntyre's thinking, the above alternatives to the authority of tradition are a tangled web of morality, which, over time, has threaded and spun its way through popular culture. It is up to the individual Christian or, in this case, the Christian parent to decide what to do in the face of this mess of sticky morality. Chrysostom's moral education, which was formed out of the theology of his age, is just one more option from which the Christian may choose as a way around the cobwebs of popular culture's moral formation.

The six streams I sketched out are not the only cultural philosophies that reject tradition, but they are prominent and interrelated. Other alternatives to tradition that still influence culture today include hedonism, intuitionism, and utilitarianism. Still, the six streams on which I focused serve to help us interpret the fragmented moral landscape described by MacIntyre. What we find when tracking down the sources of secular morality is a Pandora's box. As the Enlightenment thinkers sought to banish old demons, many new ones took their place: "One demon is exorcised, and seven others come in."[24]

As MacIntyre argues, emotivism in action is easy to find. It is indirectly in a recent work, *The Coddling of the American Mind*, which emphasizes the primacy of feelings as a major source of anxiety and depression among

---

22. Schram, "New Gnosticism."
23. Bellinger, *Trinitarian Self*, 32.
24. Bellinger, *Genealogy of Violence*, 10.

the youth.[25] Relativism, gnosticism, trendy psychology, etc., are reflected in the attitudes of individuals in and out of the church. How could these doctrines of the culture-at-large not sink into children? An example of this is in the popular children's movie *Frozen*. The animated movie is supposedly inspired by Hans Christian Andersen's *Snow Queen* but is barren of its core Christian message. The movie's alternative message is most explicit in its theme song, "Let It Go."

Pixar's *Ralph Breaks the Internet* is another example. This animated film covertly preaches that no matter who you are created to be, or what you are created for, the individual has the complete autonomy to become something else, even if it means entering into a world not designed for her. This is teaching children that they can ignore their *telos*. One basic definition that all belief systems share concerning evil is that it is *not achieving one's telos*. If this understanding is correct, then pop culture's most family-friendly movies are not safe, morally neutral forms of amusement but are, in fact, moral vehicles, smuggling heavy philosophical baggage into the minds of developing children. These examples are not here to accuse an entertainment company of ill intentions but to point out that they promote cultural values and are not neutral. These values have roots in the post-Enlightenment that lend themselves toward non-Christian systems of belief and oppose the theanthropic ethic.

To sum up this appraisal of six post-Enlightenment streams of thought, it is safe to say the error of the current age is one of anthropology. At the heart of all these beliefs is a false sense of individual autonomy that would deny the begotten nature of the human being. This unbegotten, "new Adam" is not subject to a given biology, parentage, or *telos* but can remake himself into his own image, free of gender, familial, and relational constraints. This is completely antithetical to biblical and patristic teaching.

The theanthropic ethic, which I describe in the following chapters, offers the family a defense against the pseudo-freedom that amounts to nothing more than slavery.[26] The theanthropic ethic, premodern and biblical, denies the bondage of such a "freedom" which is the doubling down of the first Adam's sin, the complete rejection of the Creator in favor of radical (and false) self-sufficiency.

Unlike Adam, the man of Genesis who was not born but made, the rest of the human race is born of parents. No matter how much the contemporary individual wishes to return to a primordial Adam-like state, this desire

---

25. Lukianoff and Haidt, *Coddling of American Mind*.

26. "Depriving people of the basic natural bonds belongs to the essence of slavery" (McCarthy, "Slavery of Radical Freedom").

tears asunder all natural bonds between father and mother, marriage and childhood. In an article appearing on the First Things website, Margaret McCarthy describes such freedom:

> Liberation from the natural bond between men and women eventually necessitates the liberation of motherhood and fatherhood from carnal bonds and the establishment of a new parenthood based on intentional, arbitrary, and contractual ones .... Liberated mothers and fathers in whatever combination, in other words, must become breeders and studs; and their liberated children, motherless and fatherless, like "Adam."

She then asks the million-dollar question, "Can we really imagine that our children will be more free by being made, not begotten, and treated like property?"[27] The new, sought-after utopia sounds more like hell on earth: complete and utter alienation from God and neighbor.

True freedom comes not with a natural Adam unrestrained by biological or relational bonds but with morality. Humans do have the freedom to choose, but the choice is between good and evil, between two models of desire, between the will of God or the will of Satan, between existence and nonexistence, between love and hate. The freedom of morality is what makes the human being godlike, different from all the other animals in creation. John Steinbeck voices this godly freedom through his character Lee: "Why, that makes a man great, that gives him stature with the gods, for in his weakness and his filth and his murder of his brother he has still the great choices. He can choose his course and fight it through and win."[28] As will be discussed in chapter 4, it is this aspect of image-bearing that disrupts nature and creates evil from nothing, when choosing radical autonomy and self-sufficiency over a relationship and participation with the Father.

I believe the error of the current age is the desire to re-create the universal order, to undermine and uproot the *Tao*.[29] It is the desire to change the world into Alice's wonderland, where "if I had a world of my own everything would be nonsense. Nothing would be what it is because everything would be what it isn't. And, contrariwise, what it is, it wouldn't be."[30] Everyone can be a Humpty Dumpty and claim, "When *I* use a word it means just what I choose it to mean—neither more nor less."[31] To resist the spirit of the

27. McCarthy, "Slavery of Radical Freedom."
28. Steinbeck, *East of Eden*, 303.
29. The Tao, as I will discuss in a later chapter, was how C. S. Lewis referred to the natural order of creation.
30. Geronimi et al., *Alice in Wonderland*.
31. Carroll, *Alice's Adventures in Wonderland*, 196.

age means to hold the lifeline of tradition that springs from Jesus Christ, to grasp the golden cord.

Below, I preview the tripart pedagogy provided by Chrysostom, which can potentially become a shield for parents to push against the alternative visions of morality examined above. In the following chapters, I show how *apatheia* cultivated through *askesis* leads to true freedom, the freedom from violent rivalry, rage, lust, and endless envy and voracious greed. I also show how biblical freedom allows for the cultivation of virtue, creative *mimesis*, and spiritual growth within the Christian family.

WHERE WE GO FROM HERE

Below is a breakdown of the following chapters, which are meant to situate and support Chrysostom's plan for the family, broadened and reconceived for the contemporary Christian parent. The explanations and descriptions provided in the following chapters are not exhaustive. The foundational theological groundwork discussed is meant to frame Chrysostom's method. One caveat to remember is that premodern Christian thinkers did not systematize theology and saw no distinction between theology and ethics, morality and spirituality. The Eastern patristic and premodern thought discussed also serves as a critique on the post-Enlightenment streams of thought, revealing these streams' overall untenable nature as a basis for Christian moral and spiritual formation. Premodern Christian thought did not develop in a vacuum—as the patristic adaptations of Greek philosophy can attest—but it is far removed from the Enlightenment effort to reduce all knowledge to empirical science.

Early Christian teaching holds faith as the purifier of human reason, not the other way around. The main patristic voice that will counter the voices of the post-Enlightenment is John Chrysostom. Secondary voices from late antiquity will include Evagrius Ponticus and those drawn from *The Philokalia*, including Maximus the Confessor. Evagrian psychology, for example, will act as a bridge between Chrysostom and Girard.

In chapter 2, I provide historical context and a short biography of John Chrysostom. In his treatise "An Address on Vainglory and the Right Way for Parents to Bring Up Their Children," Chrysostom provides his blueprint. His advice is practical, sound, and relevant despite the time, language, and cultural differences that must be bridged. His framework relies on three supporting pillars: (1) the spiritual training (*askesis*) to be practiced as a family, (2) the child's imitation of parents and spiritual elders within the church, and (3) the role of story-telling in transference of Christian virtue from one generation to the next.

Chapters 3 and 4 give the necessary theological and ethical foundation from which the theanthropic ethic can be understood. These chapters are meant to situate Chrysostom and other Eastern and desert teachers firmly within their theological framework. Chrysostom's moral and spiritual education, especially in terms of spiritual discipline, cannot be understood apart from his theology. Again, these early thinkers did not separate ethics from theology, so chapter 3 focuses on God—the Trinity, the incarnation, and other concepts related to him—concepts that deeply informed how they understood the nature of *askesis* in the process of spiritual formation.

To help bridge the gap of centuries and language, the main interpreter for Eastern Christian thought in this chapter is the theologian Vladimir Lossky. In *The Mystical Theology*, Lossky offers a lucid presentation of patristic theology. He writes, "The eastern tradition has never made a sharp distinction between mysticism and theology . . . . If the mystical experience is a personal working out of the content of the common faith, theology is an expression, for the profit of all, of that which can be experienced by everyone."[32] This statement applies to the premodern Christian view of ethics as being inseparable from theology. This undivided theology-ethic, if indeed mystical in the sense of the word Lossky uses, becomes indubitably practical and personal, permeating every aspect of life and self. There is no room for compartmentalization of life in this theology-ethic, only transformation. This discussion will be highly relevant to the contemporary understanding of Chrysostom's view of *askesis*.

To better understand this element of Chrysostom's pedagogy, I glean wisdom from *The Philokalia*. This text is an important compilation of teachings from the first millennia of Christianity. It includes the writings of Maximus the Confessor, Peter of Damasces, and many other desert fathers.

Chapter 4 picks up the study of Chrysostom's second building block: imitation. Imitation is presented as a human capacity, and therefore the chapter starts with the theological anthropology of premodern Christianity, including the doctrines of sin, death, evil. The human condition, human alienation from God, and human nature are discussed through the lens of the theanthropic ethic. Imitation, because it is a human capacity, is discussed within the context of other human capacities, as well as through the dual lenses of the fallen human condition and God's saving grace.

Much of the moral theory presented here is reliant on Stanley Harakas's understanding of Eastern theology and his work on theanthropic

---

32. Lossky, *Mystical Theology*, 8–9.

ethics, *Toward Transfigured Life*. Harakas also helps in responding to the challenges of pluralism and rapid scientific advances by noting

> it is not possible to do Christian ethics in a vacuum. The ethical thinking of non-Christian ethicists and philosophical, scientific, sociological, psychological knowledge are of necessity related to Christian ethics. This is true because Christian ethics is not a sectarian ethic. It claims to speak to all of mankind and to speak to human beings in the whole human condition.[33]

Harakas offers critiques of post-Enlightenment thinkers and schools of thought. For instance, in critiquing Fletcher's morality, he states, "It is, of course, an error to make the concrete and specific situation itself the primary feature and determinant of a given ethical decision . . . 'the situation' has numerous dimensions. It is never adequate to view the situation as *only* the immediate and concrete circumstances, though these cannot be ignored."[34] He further adds, "In the largest sense the 'situation' is the whole divine economy. The maximization of the Christ-like image—given the basic order and pattern of society—is the real 'situation' . . . the eternal situation is the relevant situation."[35]

For chapter 4's discussion of moral capacities, the work of Christian philosopher Christos Yannaras is presented. Yannaras champions the theanthropic ethic in *The Freedom of Morality*, and as a Christian existentialist he provides a counterresponse to the philosophical existentialism of Jean Paul Sartre and others closely associated with Sartre's thought like Nietzsche and Heidegger. Yannaras is similar to other existentialist thinkers in that he does not believe in the systematization of ethics, and like other Christian existentialists, he views love as "the ontological category *par excellence*."[36] Yet for any similarities to the philosophical existentialism described above, the contrast is striking when he applies the same idioms to a Christian worldview, as he does here: "Morality is not an objective measure for evaluating character and behavior, but the dynamic response of personal freedom to the existential truth and authenticity of man. . . . In other words, morality relates to the event of man's salvation . . . . The insatiable thirst common to all human existence is a thirst for this *salvation*, not for conventional improvements in character or behavior."[37]

---

33. Harakas, *Toward Transfigured Life*, 7.
34. Harakas, *Toward Transfigured Life*, 222.
35. Harakas, "Orthodox Christian Approach," 107.
36. Yannaras, *Freedom of Morality*, 18.
37. Yannaras, *Freedom of Morality*, 15–16.

Although he uses language similar to Nietzsche's, the difference between outlooks is vivid. Both thinkers value authenticity and freedom. However, Nietzsche desires freedom from the other (including all social mores and constructs, religions, other people) in order to become truly authentic, whereas Yannaras sees true human authenticity as possible only through the acceptance of God.

In the final third of the chapter, mimetic theory is discussed in terms of anthropology to provide another layer of support concerning the human capacity to learn and imitate. The next thinker, René Girard, lends credence to Chrysostom's promotion of imitation and extends the concept beyond Chrysostom. Girard's work is important because of its dual relevance: his theory spans both the nature of imitation and the nature of story-telling, myth, and literature. In his work *Things Hidden since the Foundation of the World*, Girard departs from the humanities and examines his theory of imitation through the lenses of various disciplines. This work is a significant resource for this chapter, with its focus on anthropology. Another of his books, *I See Satan Fall like Lightning*, is drawn on as the best summary of his work on mimetic theory. It also provides a compelling response to several of theanthropic ethic's challengers, particularly Nietzsche.

Chapter 4 presents positive *mimesis* through a discussion of "novelistic conversion" and extends Girard's thought into the theology of *theosis*. *Deceit, Desire and the Novel* was Girard's first major work, and it is the starting point into the theory that he continued to develop over a lifetime. As a work of literary criticism, this groundbreaking text introduced the concept of triangular desire, later to be known more widely as *mimetic desire*. Girard posits that the great novelists all capture a fundamental truth of human nature, which post-Enlightenment thinkers fail to grasp. This truth is that human beings model or imitate their desires after the desire of the other. This idea contradicts modern scholars who would have us believe that our desires are autonomous:

> They encourage the very illusion which the novel crushes, that illusion of autonomy to which modern man clings more tenaciously as it becomes increasingly false. The critics tear up the seamless tunic which the novelist has struggled to weave. They come back down to the level of common experience . . . . They reduce the novelistic work to the level of the romantic work.[38]

Girard calls this the romantic lie. Hence, the original title of the work, *Mensonge romantique et vérité Romanesque*, which translates as *The Romantic Lie and the Novelistic Truth*. Toward the end of the book, he reveals an

---

38. Girard, *Deceit, Desire*, 39–40.

uncomfortable truth, that all the great novels end in the same way: with the conversion experience of the hero:

> Every level of his existence is inverted, all the effects of metaphysical desire are replaced with contrary effects. Deception gives way to truth, anguish to remembrance, agitation to repose, hatred to love, humiliation to humility, mediated desire to autonomy, deviated transcendency to vertical transcendency. This time it is not a false but a genuine conversion. The hero triumphs in defeat; he triumphs because he is at the end of his resources; for the first time he has to look his despair and his nothingness in the face. But this look which he has dreaded, which is the death of pride, is his salvation.[39]

This concept of the "unity of novelistic conclusions" is revisited when the discussion turns to the importance of story-telling in chapter 5, as all the great novels were meant to be antidotes against the spirit of unbelief so apparent within post-Enlightenment thought. The concept of converting away from mimetic desire toward positive *mimesis* is discussed in terms of *askesis* and *theosis*.

In chapter 5, I present the story-telling aspect of Chrysostom's pedagogy. This is the third and final pillar of his structure on moral and spiritual formation. Although his discussion revolves around oral story-telling and the theater, what he says can be applied to art forms that did not exist in his day. This chapter broadens his thoughts on story-telling to include the modern art of the novel. He did not differentiate whether the story had to be heard, read, or watched. His discussion, which veers back and forth from listening to stories to watching them unfold on the stage, makes his theory amenable to all kinds of story-telling.

It is because of the malleable nature of story-telling that Alasdair MacIntyre's work can be highlighted to extend Chrysostom's thought to include all narrative. MacIntyre's definition of tradition and what he says about the "narratable life" are discussed here to flesh out the nature of Chrysostom's third element. MacIntyre's contribution provides one of the key supporting arguments on the importance of story-telling in moral formation. In the latter half of *After Virtue*, MacIntyre explains tradition, story-telling, and virtue in concrete terms. What is key is his argument for the story's use in the cultivation of virtues necessary for the survival of a tradition:

> Man is in his actions and practice, as well as in his fictions, essentially a story-telling animal. He is not essentially, but becomes

---

39. Girard, *Deceit, Desire*, 294.

through his history, a teller of stories that aspire to truth . . . . And so too of course is that moral tradition from heroic society to its medieval heirs according to which the telling of stories has a key part in educating us into the virtues.[40]

According to MacIntyre, virtues exist within specific communities of tradition. Stories are needed to retain the community's virtues, as they are the means of transferring ideas from one generation to the next. This is Chrysostom's metaphor of the "golden cord."

The vicarious nature of story-telling, as well as what sort of literature is the right kind for moral formation, is then approached through the work of Karen Swallow Prior, Joseph Bottum, Vigen Guroian, and René Girard. Vigen Guroian is helpful both in his understanding of theanthropic ethics as well as his work on children and story-telling.[41] In *Incarnate Love*, Guroian borrows from and expands on Harakas's work, offering his own critique and contributions to the discussion of theanthropic ethics. His insights here, along with his background as a Christian educator, are supportive of Chrysostom's option for moral education. An example of this can be seen in his discussion of ethics and soteriology: "The imitation of Christ is not merely the striving to attain an external model, it is an event in which *the doing is a happening* and the model is an image which transfigures from within."[42] Beyond his essays on ethics, he also wrote a helpful book on cultivating the moral imagination of the child through classic literature.

The last major thinker in this chapter is Karen Swallow Prior. Prior's book *On Reading Well* adds the idea of the vicarious experience to MacIntyre's theory of the "narratable life." Prior argues in favor of literature in the cultivation of virtue through vicarious experience. Great novels, she claims, when consumed and read carefully, can habituate the mind in the virtues. Joseph Bottum's text *The Decline of the Novel* is discussed in conjunction with Prior's book. Bottum's study on novel identifies the kinds of literary work that can be included in the category of "great novel," as used by both Prior and Girard, or "classic," as used by Guroian.

Chapter 5 concludes with an example of how story-telling can be used by the ecclesial family in the attainment of virtue and how it fits in the overall spiritual and moral life of the family. The initiatory virtue, that of obedience, is discussed and used as an example in a guided reading of C. S. Lewis's *The Silver Chair*. Finally, in the conclusion, I reemphasize the need for a holistic moral education for the Christian family.

---

40. MacIntyre, *After Virtue*, 216.
41. Guroian, *Tending the Heart*.
42. Guroian, *Incarnate Love*, 16–17.

SUMMARY

My reason in writing this book, which is deeply personal in so many ways, is to share with other Christian families the ideas, tools, and wisdom that I have gleaned in my search for answers. In essence, I want to help us all better become "little churches." Spiritual transformation is the goal. My second goal is to give a defense for the family against the anti-Christian morality that pervades Western culture. The more support the family has concerning its adversaries, the more prepared and vigilant it can be. Every Christian family has already taken a stand, just by being Christian. However, the Christian life is also a struggle, and the Christian family will always be pressured from without to conform to the norms of this world. It is time to seek hidden treasures, to call on the wisdom of the ancients, and to turn to our faith for the answers we seek.

2

St. John Chrysostom and the "Little Church"

IN ONE OF HIS homilies on marriage and family, Chrysostom exhorts, "If we regulate our households in this way, we will also be fit to oversee the church, for indeed the household is a little church."[1] This chapter will provide an in-depth examination of what Chrysostom meant by a "little church" and how the Christian character is ideally formed within the family. In the model provided within "An Address on Vainglory," Chrysostom presents three methods that should be used in raising Christian children: (1) the ascetical life, (2) the emulation of models, and (3) story-telling. The end purpose of this framework is the youth's attainment of Christian character. Yet before delving into his concept of moral and spiritual education, it is beneficial to situate Chrysostom within the remarkable company of fellow teachers who preceded or lived contemporaneously with him. These additional voices will reveal what the common Christian teaching concerning the family was during the first four centuries of the church.

I am not interested in simply restating the contents of "On Vainglory." I wish to offer not only a historical review of Chrysostom but to see his thought juxtaposed next to contemporary thinkers who share a similar understanding of human nature and moral formation. If MacIntyre is correct

---

1. Chrysostom, *On Marriage*, 57.

that Western society has suffered a moral apocalypse—and I believe he is—then it is time to go back to the earliest Christian moral teachings on moral growth. In the following pages, the proverbial toe is dipped into the stream of history and tradition flowing from the original fount of the first four centuries of Christian teaching. Chrysostom's blueprint is not a one-size-fits-all scheme to impose on all families. Instead, his "golden cord" is an educational pattern that can be used only within a certain type of community (Christian) that makes this moral framework possible. To understand this community, history, and tradition, I step back and consider how the early church fathers wrestled with Scripture, the questions they asked, and how they were challenged by the writings of the apostles. Below, I will discuss the challenges and responses of some of Chrysostom's peers—including Athanasius, the Cappadocian fathers, Jerome, and others—to gain a sense of how they struggled with the biblical texts on children and Christian education.

EARLY CHRISTIANS ON EDUCATION

From the very beginning, Christians were concerned with how to raise their children in Christlikeness. They paid special attention to the apostle Paul's exhortation, "Children, obey your parents in the Lord, for this is right. 'Honor your father and mother' (this is the first commandment with a promise), 'that it may go well with you and that you may live long in the land.' Fathers, do not provoke your children to anger, but bring them up in the discipline and instruction of the Lord" (Eph 6:1–4). These four verses near the end of the epistle to the church of Ephesus were the starting place for creating a moral and spiritual framework for instructing children in the faith.

Early Christian documents reveal how some early Christian teachers attempted to answer the question of discipleship and children. What I find is an emphasis on the parents' obligation toward their young, as seen in the earliest extant Christian sermon: "As a reward I beg of you to repent with all your heart and give to yourselves salvation and life. For if we do this, we shall set a mark for all the young who wish to work in the cause of piety and the goodness of God."[2] However, other than brief statements such as this one, the question of Christian education for the young is largely ignored until Chrysostom. An example is seen in the so-called *Teaching of the Twelve Apostles*, or *The Didache*, which was an ancient didactic text from the third century. This early writing references the children of Christians in one brief

---

2. Second Clement 19: 1, as quoted in Laistner, *Christianity and Pagan Culture*, 30. The author and place of origin of 2 Clement is unknown, and the manuscript is dated between AD 120 and 150 (Drobner, *Fathers of the Church*, 57–58).

sentence: "You shall not withhold your hand from your son or daughter, but from their youth you shall teach them the fear of God."[3]

This exhortation is repeated and developed in another early Christian text. Contemporaneous with Chrysostom is the compilation of the *Constitutions of the Holy Apostles*. The first six books, including the passage below, are based on an obscure anonymous Greek text, *Didascalia Apostolorum*, which was written sometime in the third century. The second section of book 4 provides an interpretation of Ephesians 6:1–4:

> Ye fathers, educate your children in the Lord, bringing them up in the nurture and admonition of the Lord; and teach them such trades as are agreeable and suitable to the word, lest they by such opportunity become extravagant, and continue without punishment from their parents, and so get relaxation before their time, and go astray from that which is good. Wherefore be not afraid to reprove them, and to teach them wisdom with severity. For your corrections will not kill them, but rather preserve them.[4]

This is not a pedagogy with a theory on spiritual formation. As the text continues, the emphasis is corporeal punishment. The author is concerned about children who grow up with lenient parents, as the child might take "mastery" over the parents or see them as equals. This lack of respect for authority means a lack of respect for God and his commandments. This leads to all kinds of sinful behavior, according to the author, for which the parent will have to account to God.

There are some similarities between this admonition and Chrysostom's pastoral writings on childrearing. The implication in this text and Chrysostom's teachings is that their audience is affluent, more given to spoiling their children. Why else would the child have the time for relaxation "and to go astray"? *The Didache*, however, is more generic, with its brief statement on discipline. It gives us no hint of a wealthy audience, which is probably why the writer did not need to go into great detail on the form and nature of discipline. Nonetheless, both third-century documents give Christian teaching for parents that can be applied, at least in spirit, by modern parents. Simply calling for more discipline and punishment for children, however, does not speak to the spiritual life of the whole family.

---

3. Huleatt, *Two Ways*, 6.
4. *Constitutions of Holy Apostles*, bk 4, §2, ch. 9.

St. Clement of Alexandria

Another Christian father interested in the discipleship of the young was St. Clement of Alexandria. Clement lived sometime between AD 140 to 215, over a century before Chrysostom was active in his ministry. He wrote *Christ the Educator* to teach the newly baptized how to live in Christ. Jesus is presented as the pedagogue, the slave who led the young boy to school and taught him right conduct. The pedagogue did not teach the child the ABCs; that was the schoolteacher's job. Instead, the pedagogue's purpose was to teach *how to live*. He instructed his charge in manners, behavior, and the correct attitude toward others in society. In Clement's metaphor, the baptized are the school children, Jesus Christ their pedagogue: "The pedagogue, then, is of course the Logos, who leads the children, that is, us (*paidas . . . agōn*), to salvation."[5]

Clement's pastoral efforts in writing this guide show that the desire to teach young Christians was not a new concern by Chrysostom's day. Although Clement was writing to new converts, his work in *Christ the Educator* is a good place to start a discussion on Christian spiritual education in the family. Seeing that another early church father viewed Jesus as the ultimate teacher who guided the formation of the spirit in his pupils shows Chrysostom is rooted in a vibrant and shared tradition. Chrysostom's vision of Christian education was first proposed to his Antiochian congregation some 150 years after Clement.

St. Athanasius and Christian Fellowship

How the great fathers of the church understood the Christian life is helpful as the broader context for understanding the stream of ideas on which Chrysostom drew for his pedagogy. After Clement, the next teacher to whom to look is St. Athanasius the Great (ca. AD 295 to 373), who is known as the defender of Nicene Christianity. Right living for Athanasius is intimately linked with the incarnation, as recalled by the famous declaration that God became human that humans might become divine.[6] Athanasius understood that for the Christian moral life, virtue is cultivated through imitation of those who know the way, i.e., spiritually mature Christians. Transformation is the result of this union with the body of Christ, the community of Christ followers who incarnate (re)new(ed) humanity. The one who joins this

---

5. Clement, *Christ the Educator*, 1.53.3, as quoted in Moreschini and Norelli, *Early Christian*, 255.

6. Athanasius, *Incarnation*, 54.

company, which Athanasius viewed as the fellowship of life, is enabled to be transformed by this "ontological union in virtue."[7] For Athanasius, a person never gains true virtue outside of salvation in Christ. Only those who enter the community with the right *telos* and right guides can attain true virtue. This community is the church.

The Cappadocians

Three important teachers who lived and worked during the same era as Chrysostom are the Cappadocians. As with Athanasius, virtue is a recurrent theme in the works of these three prodigious theologians. The brothers St. Basil of Caesarea (ca. AD 329 to 379) and St. Gregory of Nyssa (ca. AD 335 to 394) came from a Christian family known to produce great teachers on the Christian life. Their friend St. Gregory Nazianzus (ca. AD 326 to 390) praised their parents and family in a funeral oration, calling them "admirers of virtue" and "inspiration to virtue" even during times of persecution.[8] All three teachers—Gregory of Nyssa, Basil of Caesarea, and Gregory Nazianzus—emphasized the life of true virtue in Christ—"Certainly whoever pursues true virtue participates in nothing other than God, because he is himself absolute virtue"[9]—and adapted the Greek classical mode of education, the *paideia*, into a Christian "basic training."[10]

An example of this adaptation is Basil's "Address to Young Men on Reading Greek Literature." In this letter-treatise, Basil instructs students on the way to discriminate what to retain from their classical education and what should be abandoned as false.[11] *Eudaimonia* and the purpose of life for the Christian is found in Scripture and taught in the sacramental life of the church. What the ancient Greek poets and writers offer toward the praise of virtue, and what is in harmony with Scripture, can be kept. This retention became the basis of natural law theory in the Christian East.

---

7. Woodill, *Fellowship of Life*, 16.
8. Nazianzen, *Funeral Orations*, 27–28.
9. Gregory of Nyssa, *Life of Moses*, 31.
10. Woodill, *Fellowship of Life*, 21.
11. The letter-treatise was a Christian literary genre by the fourth century. These were long doctrinal letters that covered a variety of theological topics (Moreschini and Norelli, *Early Christian*, 94).

Two Letters from St. Jerome

The next significant teacher on the subject of spiritual and moral education is St. Jerome. In Jerome, we have one more Christian voice on the education of children, albeit with a narrower focus that does not apply to all Christian children but to girls and young women. Between his two letters to the virgins Eustochium and Demetrias, Jerome gives his advice on spiritual discipline: "Love to occupy your mind with the reading of Scripture. Do not in the good ground of your breast gather only a crop of darnel [a ryegrass] and wild oats. Do not let an enemy sow tares among the wheat when the householder is asleep."[12] While advice like this is good for any Christian, Jerome's view of married life with childbearing is that it is a lesser arena for growing into Christlikeness, one that is less meaningful and desirable to the Christian compared to the life of celibacy devoted to God:

> I write to you thus, Lady Eustochium (I am bound to call my Lord's bride '*lady*'), to show you by my opening words that my object is not to praise the virginity which you follow, and of which you have proved the value, or yet to recount the drawbacks of marriage, such as pregnancy, the crying of infants, the torture caused by a rival, the cares of household management, and all those fancied blessings which death at last cuts short. Not that married women are as such outside the pale; they have their own place, the marriage that is honorable and the bed undefiled.[13]

His tone and attitude toward marriage and children leave little that can be used in reference to Christian family life, and his sentiments on marriage are the opposite of Chrysostom's, since Chrysostom viewed the fruit of marriage as more than "drawbacks" or "fancied blessings" but real blessings from God. Still, through Jerome, Christians are given another view of a possible life in Christ, one that has its lessons and benefits. As this is not a discussion on the single life, however, Jerome's two letters are highlighted simply to show the extent of literature in early Christianity that touched on Christian education of the young.

THE LIFE OF ST. JOHN CHRYSOSTOM

None of the church fathers up to this point devoted as much time preaching and writing on the Christian education of the young as Chrysostom.

---

12. Jerome, "Letter 130," §7, in *Jerome*, 265.
13. Jerome, "Letter 22," §2, in *Jerome*, 23.

Yet their writings illustrate that Christians were invested in the question of rearing the young in the faith from the very beginning. Clement of Alexandria emphasizes the education of the new convert, Athanasius writes of transformation into Christlikeness, and the Cappadocians stress virtuous living. Chrysostom, more of a pastor than a theologian, drew on all of these teachings to create a blueprint, or guide, for parents to follow. Before examining his work on the education of the young, a short biography will give us an idea of his personality, character, and the historical context of his life.

Chrysostom was born to an aristocratic and wealthy family of Antioch around the year AD 348.[14] In this way, his life parallels the three Cappadocian fathers, as the wealth of their respective families allowed them the advantages of higher education. Also similar was the fact that these men were encouraged and directed by the women in their lives to pursue Christian vocations: Basil and Gregory of Nyssa by their sister, St. Macrina the Younger; Gregory of Nazianzus by his mother, Nonna; and Chrysostom also by his mother. Chrysostom's father, Secundus, died while Chrysostom was a child, leaving his wife, Anthusa, a widow by twenty.[15] Anthusa was a devout Christian. She decided to remain a widow, thereby dedicating her life to God, and to give her son the best education possible for the time.[16] Chrysostom was taught by tutors of rhetoric, including Libanius, in the Greek classical tradition—the same *paideia* critiqued by Basil—alongside biblical instruction. Libanius was a famous rhetor who drew many students, including Theodore of Mopsuestia, who studied with Chrysostom.

Upon his baptism in 372, Chrysostom wished to further his theological education. He entered the *asketerion* of Diodore of Tarsus to learn biblical exegesis. A few years into his studies, he became a lector. In a desire to further his spiritual formation through *askesis*, Chrysostom then moved into another monastic community near Antioch. After four years, he entered a hermitage, where he memorized a large portion of the Bible. However, in two years, he had to abandon his life in the wilderness. The intensity of his ascetical struggles left him in fragile health and forced him back to the city.

Once in Antioch, Chrysostom entered the ecclesiastic life, and in 381, Bishop Meletius consecrated him a deacon. As a deacon, he served the poor, orphans, widows, and virgins. Part of his service included the education of

---

14. The actual date of his birth is unknown, but the approximate range is between AD 344 and 354.

15. Drobner, *Fathers of the Church*, 327.

16. In the fourth century, Roman law changed to permit mothers to have guardianship of their children instead of a male custodian as long as the mother remained a widow. This is how Anthusa was able to determine her son's education (see Harlow and Laurence, *Cultural History of Childhood*).

children, which gave him the experience and insight seen in his treatise on the subject. It was during this period that he was first noted for his brilliant ability in rhetoric and the pastoral nature of his writings. Five years later, on February 28, 386, Bishop Flavian ordained him a priest, intent on seeing Chrysostom embark on a preaching ministry. During these years in Antioch, Chrysostom preached his greatest homilies and, among these, is noted for his themes of marriage and family as the "ecclesial locus for the formation of virtue."[17] According to his theology of marriage and family, these were the arenas in which the majority of Christians (as opposed to the minority who would take up a life of singlehood) would be formed into the image of Christ. It is this theology, found abundantly in his homilies, that I will analyze and describe.

After twelve years as a priest in Antioch, his life changed dramatically, when the patriarch of Constantinople, Nectarius, died. The Emperor Arcadius, upon the advice of his minister Eutopius, appointed Chrysostom to be the new patriarch. Chrysostom was kidnapped and secreted out of Antioch, lest the Antiochians prevent their favorite preacher from leaving the city. So, in 398, he was led to Constantinople and was ordained bishop.

The last six years of his life as bishop were not easy on Chrysostom. For one, he was a gifted orator but a terrible diplomat. He did not fit in at the imperial court due to his uncompromising Christian ethic. Unlike his predecessor Nectarius, who had been a gifted politician, Chrysostom was simply a good pastor. The people came to love him for his fearless preaching, but he made enemies within church and government when he spoke out against the corruption and laxity of both. A century later, one historian noted this aspect of Chrysostom's preaching: "John attracted the admiration of the people, while he strenuously expiated against sin, and testified the same indignation against all acts of injustice as if they had been perpetuated against him. This boldness pleased the common people, but grieved the wealthy and the powerful, who were guilty of most of the vices he denounced."[18] Chrysostom's attempts to reform the corrupt clergy made him bitter and powerful enemies, including the first minister, Eutopius, who had been responsible for his rise to the patriarchy.

His honesty and lack of political acumen had not been dangerous in Antioch, but in Constantinople, the seat of imperial power in the East, these traits proved perilous. A combination of events managed to stoke the fires against Chrysostom. First, Eutopius fell from grace, and Chrysostom granted his enemy asylum, and then he did likewise to a group of monks who were

---

17. Woodill, *Fellowship of Life*, 25.
18. Sozomen et al., *Ecclesiastical History*, 363.

accused of heresy. Although Chrysostom did the latter only to undertake an investigation into the charge, he angered both Bishop Theophilus and Bishop Epiphanius, and they turned against him. Lastly, Empress Eudoxia took a personal dislike to Chrysostom for his sermons against extravagant living. For instance, in his "Homily 48 on Matthew," he identifies Christ with the poor and criticizes those wealthy who refuse to share with the needy out of their abundance:

> You eat in excess; Christ eats not even what he needs. You eat a variety of cakes; he eats not even a piece of dried bread. You drink fine Thracian wine; but on him you have not bestowed so much as a cup of cold water. You lie on a soft and embroidered bed; but he is perishing in the cold.... You live in luxury on things that properly belong to him.... At the moment, you have taken possessions of the resources that belong to Christ and you consume them aimlessly. Don't you realize that you are going to be held accountable?[19]

Like Athanasius, who was banished five times and spent seventeen years in exile, Chrysostom's efforts on behalf of the church were not well received. His enemies, including Theophilus, relieved him of office in 403, and he avoided exile this time only because of happenstance. When he continued to preach in his usual fashion, the emperor ordered him out of the city in 404. In his last sermon, he left his congregation with these words:

> The waters are raging, and the winds are blowing, but I have no fear for I stand firmly upon a rock. What am I to fear? Is it death? Life to me means Christ, and death is gain. Is it exile? The earth and everything it holds belongs to the Lord. Is it loss of property? I brought nothing into this world, and I will bring nothing out of it. I have only contempt for the world and its ways, and I scorn its honors.[20]

Chrysostom did not go without a fight, at first ignoring the order, but he was eventually forced by the emperor's soldiers to Cucusus in Armenia, where he stayed for three years. From exile, he wrote 240 letters. These letters attest that he still bore some ecclesial influence, as is shown in this correspondence with Innocent:

> We have deemed it necessary to persuade my lords, the most honoured and pious bishops Demetrius, Pansophius, Papus and Eugenius to leave their own churches, and venture on this

---

19. Chrysostom, *Homilies on the Gospel*, 301.
20. Volz, "Genius of Chrysostom's Preaching."

great sea voyage, and set out on a long journey from home, and hasten to your Charity, and, after informing you clearly of everything, to make measures for redressing the evils as speedily as possible.[21]

In response to this threat, his political enemies successfully encouraged the emperor to banish him to the remote Pityus, for fear of his continued influence over church affairs. It was this last, treacherous journey that stressed his already deteriorating health, and he died of exhaustion on September 14, 407.

Through the appeals of Pope Innocent, Chrysostom's reputation was restored posthumously in 412. On January 27, 438, his body was returned to Constantinople, and he was interred. Only then was he given the title, which is so familiar today, of "golden-mouth." He is now recognized as one of the four "doctors" of the Eastern church, in the company of Athanasius, Basil the Great, and Gregory of Nazianzus.

St. John Chrysostom's Pedagogy

The work of greatest interest for this topic is the panegyric discourse entitled "An Address on Vainglory and the Right Way for Parents to Bring Up Their Children."[22] A panegyric is like a homily, as it is a public address meant to teach. In the case of the panegyric, it was meant to be preached at a celebration. Chrysostom's panegyric was preached during a feast. "On Vainglory" was written for this purpose around the year 393, not long before Chrysostom left Antioch. It was the first half of a treatise entitled *On the Education of Sons*, one of the few documents of this era on Christian education, the other being Basil's letter-treatise on the reading of pagan classics.

Two manuscripts of this panegyric have survived, both of which were copied around the end of the tenth century. The translations of these are not included in the compilations of his vast corpus due to the question of their authenticity. Doubts concerning the origins of these manuscripts were laid to rest, however, after the thorough work of S. Haidacher in 1907.[23] Haidacher not only proved this treatise was genuine and not the work of later editors but used his in-depth knowledge and familiarity of Chrysostom's

---

21. Chrysostom, "Correspondence of St. Chrysostom with the Bishop of Rome," in *On the Priesthood*, 309.

22. The critical edition of this work is Chrysostom and Malingrey, *Sur la vaine gloire*.

23. Laistner, *Christianity and Pagan Culture*, 76.

writings to show by example that "On Vainglory" had all the characteristics and idiosyncrasies one could expect from the same author.

The retrieval of this text is important not only for Christian scholarship but for the pastoral nature of the content. This document is Chrysostom's blueprint for the Christian education of children and the purpose of parenting.

The Aim of Parenthood

The first important point to understand regarding Chrysostom's theology is that the "little church" begins with the marriage between husband and wife. Chrysostom saw marriage as one of two arenas of life where the Christian could attain Christlikeness, the other being that of the celibate. Unlike Augustine, he did not view marriage's primary *telos* as procreation.[24] Childbearing was a secondary end, a blessing and outpouring of God's grace on the marriage, but the marriage itself was the vessel of spiritual formation, as together and in solidarity man and woman move toward participation with God in Christ:

> St. Paul tells us to seek peace and the sanctification without which it is impossible to see the Lord. So whether we presently live in virginity, in our first marriage, or in our second, let us pursue holiness, that we may be counted worthy to see Him and to attain the Kingdom of Heaven, through the grace and love for mankind of our Lord Jesus Christ, to whom be glory, dominion, and honor, with the Father and the Holy Spirit, now and ever, and unto ages of ages. Amen.[25]

As for parents, Chrysostom believed their God-given goal was to grow in grace and likewise guide their children in spiritual formation, for the sake of God's kingdom. The family, as with the marriage, is meant to be transfigured through life in Christ, manifesting life and God's kingdom in a dying and fallen world. The influences and temptations of the world present stumbling blocks to overcome.

Like the current moral climate, Chrysostom lived in a time of moral decline, cultural Christianity, and a population preoccupied with material wealth, entertainment, and upward mobility. He worried about the Christian parents in his congregation who desired the worldly success of their

---

24. "Some writers, especially those in the tradition of St. Augustine of Hippo, have spread the opinion that sexual relations are evil in themselves but tolerated within marriage for the purpose of procreation" (Catherine P. Roth, in Chrysostom, *On Marriage*, 9).

25. Chrysostom, *On Marriage*, 42.

offspring at the expense of spiritual well-being. "If a child learns a trade, or is highly educated for a lucrative profession, all this is nothing compared to the art of detachment from riches; if you want to make your child rich, teach him this. He is truly rich who does not desire great possessions, or surround himself with wealth, but who requires nothing."[26] He explains further,

> Don't surround [your children] with the external safeguards of wealth and fame, for when these fail—and they will fail—our children will stand naked and defenseless, having gained no profit from their former prosperity, but only injury, since when those artificial protections that shield them from the winds are removed, they will be blown to the ground in a moment. Therefore wealth is a hindrance, because it leaves us unprepared for the hardships of life.[27]

His homilies, treatise, and letters describe the Christian life, or discipleship, as the key to how parents are to assume responsibility for the moral growth of the young. He holds a Trinitarian understanding of the family as mother, father, and child. The mother and father are to emulate God the Father in his love for the Son, and the child likewise is to model the obedience and love of Jesus as the Son, to the Father through the Holy Spirit. This is the little church, or the ecclesial family.

Chrysostom's favorite metaphor for this Christian ecclesial family is expressed in his homily on Ephesians 6:1–4. He likens parents to painters or sculptors, and children to the canvas or marble. It is the task of the painter to reveal the true likeness of his subject matter, and thus the task of the mother and father to reveal more and more, little by little, the true likeness of God in their children, while the child is under their care. Chrysostom urged, "To each of you fathers and mothers, I say, just as we see artists fashioning their paintings and statues with great precision, so we must care for these wondrous statues of ours.... Like the creators of statues so you give all your leisure to fashioning these wondrous statues for God."[28]

Chrysostom also speaks harshly to parents who neglect to correct and nurture the spiritual development in their children, using the priest Eli from 1 Samuel as a prime example. "For not even Eli himself was one of those in great degree qualified to form [Samuel]; (how could he be, he who was not able to form even his own children?) No, it was the faith of the mother and her earnest zeal that wrought the whole."[29] He saw this type of neglect

---

26. Chrysostom, *On Marriage*, 68–69.
27. Chrysostom, *On Marriage*, 71.
28. Chrysostom, as quoted in Guroian, "Ecclesial Family," 69.
29. Chrysostom, "Homily 21," in *Homilies on Ephesians*, 154.

as fundamentally a failure to love the neighbor, as children are the closest neighbor to the parent. The neglect of the child's spiritual formation imperiled the child's soul. Chrysostom also thought that parents who put their own needs before the needs of their children were worse than parents who outright killed their children.[30]

There is a soteriological element to Chrysostom's theology of the ecclesial family. As I noted above in his theology of marriage, Chrysostom believed the parents needed to be personally virtuous, fully participating in the life of the church in their own growth toward Christlikeness. As with his example of the high priest Eli, however, he viewed otherwise virtuous parents who failed to bring their children up in "the discipline and instruction of the Lord" as deceived. Their personal goodness did not count for much, as in the end they would be judged by God for how they raised their children.[31] He even drew on the parable of the talents to flesh out this idea, likening the parents to the servant who buried the money given into his care instead of investing it for his master's future use. The parents' task is to prepare their children for membership and life in the kingdom of God. If they do not, the salvation of both child and parent is at stake. As he preached in his Ephesians homily:

> Let this then be our task, to mold and direct both ourselves and [our children] according to what is right. Otherwise with what sort of boldness shall we stand before the judgment-seat of Christ? If a man who has unruly children is unworthy to be a Bishop [Titus 1:6], much more is he unworthy of the kingdom of Heaven. What do you say? If we have an unruly wife, or unruly children, shall we have to render account? Yes, we shall, if we do not with exactness bring in that which is due from ourselves; for our own individual virtue is not enough in order to salvation. If the man who laid aside one talent gained nothing, but was punished even in such a manner, it is plain that one's own virtue is not enough in order to salvation, but there is need of that of another also. Let us therefore entertain with great solicitude for our wives, and take great care of our children, and of our servants, and of ourselves. And in our government both of ourselves and of them, let us beseech God that He aid us in the work.[32]

---

30. Gurioan, "Ecclesial Family," 72–73.
31. Gurioan, "Ecclesial Family," 72–73.
32. Chrysostom, "Homily 21," in *Homilies on Ephesians*, 157.

How do the parents educate themselves and accomplish such a task? Chrysostom did not leave his congregation in any doubt, giving several answers to this question on the pattern of life for the Christian family.

STEP ONE: THE ASCETICAL LIFE

The first answer to parents is his appeal for them to practice and teach the spiritual disciplines to their children. Statements like the following are made throughout "On Vainglory": "Teach thy son to be sober and vigilant and to shorten sleep for the sake of prayer, and with every word and deed to set upon himself the seal of faith."[33] To Chrysostom, the ascetical life is not a requirement reserved for the monk but a necessary component to every Christian life. Here is the beginning of sanctification, the dying to the self in submission and cooperation with the activity of the Holy Spirit.[34] Chrysostom knew the parents in his congregation in Antioch could not lead their children into the Syrian desert for six years to learn to control their passions, as he once did. Yet he did not exempt them from the purpose of *askesis* and held them to the same standard as every other Christian: the need to slay the flesh.[35]

For the ecclesial family, this means a double duty. Parents must learn self-control and cultivate Christian virtue and at the same time guide children through the struggle toward dispassion and growth in holiness. This means the vocation of parenthood is actually more heroic than that of the monk, for the monk has less distraction to encumber his struggle than that of the parent! Singleness is a gift, in this sense. The Christian parent has to go beyond both the Christian solitary and the secular parent, which indeed calls for a level of heroism, if heroism be another term for the meekness and humility necessary to submit to God's active operations on the soul.[36]

---

33. Chrysostom, "Address on Vainglory," 96. This is one example of how Chrysostom stresses ascetical practice in the rearing of children. If we consider that the original use of the Greek work ἄσκησις was in reference to athletes, then Chrysostom's exhortation to raise athletes for Christ recalls this original meaning and broadens it to include the spiritual nature of the child.

34. In cooperation as a "fellow worker" with the Holy Spirit. "We are God's fellow workers [συνεργοί]," Paul writes in 1 Cor 3:9. I am writing from the perspective of the Eastern tradition that holds to the synergism of the early church as opposed to the monogism of Reformation theology.

35. ἄσκησις means "exercise, practice, training"(Liddell, et al., *Greek-English Lexicon*, 257).

36. Which is why Chrysostom spends so much time on vainglory, the opposite of humility.

In a sense, parents must be the spiritual pioneers of their family, just as the apostle Paul was a spiritual pioneer of the church to the Corinthians. As William Goff notes in his *Dynamic Discipleship*, "Paul is being very 'gutsy' in saying to them, in effect, 'You follow me. I will not let you down. You can count on me to show you how this Christian faith works; how prayer and love and forgiveness work. I will not let you down.'"[37] A Christian parent is the child's first encounter with Christ. Indeed, this parent, too, must be "gutsy." It is not happenstance that Paul uses parenthood as a metaphor in 1 Corinthians 4:14–17:

> I do not write these things to make you ashamed, but to admonish you as my beloved children. For though you have countless guides in Christ, you do not have many fathers. For I became your father in Christ Jesus through the gospel. I urge you, then, be imitators of me. That is why I sent you Timothy, my beloved and faithful child in the Lord, to remind you of my ways in Christ, as I teach them everywhere in the church.

Vainglory as an Obstacle to Virtue in the Little Church

What constitutes the main struggle toward dispassion for parents is the subject matter of the first section of Chrysostom's "On Vainglory," in which he deals with the sin translated as the old-fashioned word *vainglory*. In contemporary parlance, vainglory is a kind of self-esteem. How strange this sounds to modern ears! Self-esteem is an obstacle to moral and spiritual growth in children? This is the exact opposite of what the current therapeutic culture would teach on the matter of child-rearing. A premodern Christian definition of vainglory is provided by John Climacus (ca. AD 579 to 649) who served as a monk, abbot, and writer of instructional material for Christians. In his understanding of virtue and vice, as presented in *The Ladder of Divine Ascent*, Climacus sees vainglory as "a perversion of character"[38] in the one who has made progress in the struggle, "only to turn the progress into a narrative of self-worth."[39] Thus, vainglory is a type of pride, one that accompanies the struggle for virtue, in which the moral agent begins to tell herself that she is the one who has achieved this change, not God. It is the one who forgets God's grace is the transformer and shaper of hearts, and man is the lesser partner in this cooperative effort.

---

37 Goff, *Dynamic Discipleship*, 32.
38. John Climacus, as quoted in Woodill, *Fellowship of Life*, 46.
39 Woodill, *Fellowship of Life*, 46.

Returning to Chrysostom's teachings and why he would treat vainglory as the main obstacle to the little church's progress, M. L. W. Laistner helpfully provides some explanation in the introduction to his English translation of "On Vainglory," writing, "He [Chrysostom] regarded vainglory as at the root of the moral and social evils which his system of education was meant to remedy."[40] Chrysostom begins his treatise addressing this obstacle first and, only after describing the problem, moves into the second half of his essay to give an account of the right way Christian parents are to educate their children to the Lord.

Chrysostom personifies vainglory, whom he calls an evil spirit, and describes this spirit as an attractive and jewel-adorned prostitute. He also uses the metaphor of a tempting fruit, "the fruit of Sodom." The temptation of this fruit/temptress causes those tempted to wish to be perceived as virtuous, successful, generous, wealthy, and philanthropic. A good reputation is highly prized by this person. The one tempted into vainglory also wants to hear praise. He wants his accomplishments to be recognized by his neighbors.

It is easy to see how this vice might trip up parents. Is it not always a temptation for a parent to be recognized as a "good" parent, a parent who provides the child with everything: a good education; fashionable clothing; expensive toys; and showy, extravagant birthday parties? This can manifest itself in extracurricular activities, as exemplified by the obnoxious Little League father yelling at the coach from the sidelines or the "dance mom" who pushes her daughter to outshine the other little children at the recital. Chrysostom describes this kind of attitude to his congregation in a humorous way:

> The man-child has lately been born. His father thinks of every means, not whereby he may direct the child's life wisely, but whereby he may adorn it and clothe it in fine raiment and golden ornaments. Why dost thou this, O man? Granted that thou dost thyself wear these, why dost thou rear in this luxury thy son who is as yet still ignorant of this folly? For what purpose dost thou put a necklet about his throat? There is need for a strict tutor to direct the boy, no need for gold. And thou lettest his hair hang down behind, thereby at once making him look effeminate and like a girl and softening the ruggedness of his sex. Implanting in him from the first an excessive love of wealth and teaching him to be excited by things of no profit, why dost thou plot even greater treachery against him? . . . Many may laugh at what I am saying on the ground that these are trifles. They are not trifles

40. Laistner, *Christianity and Pagan Culture*, 76.

but of the first importance. The girl who has been reared in her mother's quarters to be excited by female ornaments, when she leaves her father's house will be a sore vexation to her bridegroom and a greater burden to him than the tax collectors.[41]

By this description, it is easy to see how vainglory distorts parenthood and obscures the *telos* by disordering the parents' priorities. Are the mother or father doing these things for the sake of the child or for the sake of appearances? If the former, then the end goal has been lost in lesser substitutes. If the latter, then the self-interest on the parent's part replaces self-giving and sacrificial love for the child. Chrysostom wanted to dispel the lies of vainglory and provide an antidote to the afflicted parent.

Spiritual Exercise

Now that Chrysostom's understanding of parenthood is clear, I can now speak to the subsequent temptation of vainglory as the chief obstacle in virtue training. The first element of this tripart education, spiritual practice (*askesis*), can now be defined and described. However, *askesis* cannot be understood apart from the *pathos* that is translated as "passion" in English. For the ancient world, "passion" did not have the connotation that it has today, evoking emotions, creativity, and freedom. In fact, it meant the very opposite to the ancients. The passions are impulses of the soul (or heart and body), which are suffered passively. In other words, they are impulses, addictions, cravings, etc., to which the human being is in bondage. This is the "*domination* of the soul bound up in something other than the heart borne up in the love of God."[42] The passion itself can be an otherwise positive or neutral impulse that is distorted or misdirected into taking on a negative form, one that enslaves the soul. The current obsession with health seen today can be viewed as a passion, as a distorted good.

Askesis, which involves *agona* (struggle), is undergoing spiritual practice to achieve freedom from the passions and the attainment of Christlikeness, in that order. If the Christian cannot serve two masters, then the struggle against the passions is one of life and death and one of re-creation. Jesus already freed the sinner from sin and death, making this transformation possible. Working with and being aided by the Holy Spirit, Chrysostom and the other church fathers saw sanctification not as something achieved at

---

41. Chrysostom, "Address on Vainglory," 93–94.
42. Steenberg, *Beginnings of a Life*, 37.

the instant of conversion but, instead, "accomplished through a lifetime of constant striving and maturing."[43]

The ascetic struggle, often associated with monasticism, is seen throughout the entirety of Scripture, both Hebrew and Christian, and reaffirmed by Jesus Christ in the Gospel triad of prayer, fasting, and almsgiving. These are the ways in which the Christian dies to the self, learns self-control, and is freed from the impulses and addictions that keep the disciple from the attainment of Christlike virtue. As one writer puts it, "Life in Christ *is* virtue."[44]

What does Chrysostom have to say on *askesis*, especially in response to the obstacle of vainglory? The answer is basic, and he repeats it in various ways, using a variety of metaphors to help his audience grasp his point. He explicitly writes, "Let him [the child] also learn to fast.... Let him visit the church ... let him learn to pray with great fervor and contrition ... if he fasts and prays, all this is a sufficient guide to virtue."[45] One definition of almsgiving is that it is also a kind of prayer and fast. The almsgiver is offering a sacrifice of self to God just as she does so in prayer and fasting. Chrysostom reiterates Jesus' commands to pray, fast, and give, all of which allow one to die to self and be reimaged in the likeness of Christ.

Chrysostom liked to provide metaphors to help his listeners grasp the purpose of the spiritual exercises, and two of these were the athlete and the city. "Raise up an athlete for Christ! and teach him though he is in the world to be reverent from his earliest youth."[46] The athlete must be trained, coached, molded, and taught to endure physical pain as the body is transformed into its best possible state. "Regard thyself as a king ruling over a city which is the soul of thy son; for the soul is in truth a city. And, even as in a city some are thieves and some are honest men, some work steadily and some transact their business fitfully, so it is with the thoughts and reasoning in the soul."[47] Chrysostom goes on to describe this city, which needs laws to guide its members, soldiers to battle on its behalf, walls to protect it, and so on. His use of basic psychology is also instructive. He emphasizes the five senses, likening them to the gates of a city closed against those who would come through the gates to ransack and destroy.

---

43. Guroian, *Incarnate Love*, 16.
44. Woodill, *Fellowship of Life*, 17.
45. Guroian, "Ecclesial Family," 118–19.
46. Chrysostom, "Address on Vainglory," 95.
47. Chrysostom, "Address on Vainglory," 96.

STEP TWO: IMITATION

After *askesis* comes the second building block in St. John's vision of moral formation: imitation. Chrysostom puts it succinctly when he says, "Nothing, yea nothing, is so effective as emulation."[48] Emulation, he goes on to elaborate, "is a more potent instrument than fear or promises or aught else."[49] In this passage, Chrysostom is advising parents of teenagers to point out to their children other teenagers who refrain from visiting the theater, advising, "Let us point out any of his companions who are holding back from this [the theater], so that he may be held fast in the grip of emulation."[50]

The term used by Chrysostom for emulation is the Greek *zelous* and *zelotupía*, which evokes the emotion of jealousy, the desire to be like another.[51] This idea of emulation is part of Chrysostom's basic psychology. In this respect, his concept of moral formation agrees with contemporary ideas on how children learn moral behavior. Emulation involves copying another, a model, and parallels contemporary strides taken in scholarship over the importance of *mimesis*, or imitation, in learning. Chrysostom, writing nearly seventeen centuries before the discovery of mirror neurons, relied on the inspiration of Scripture, his experience as a veteran pastor, and the guidance of the Holy Spirit. He spoke a truth that modern science is late to acknowledge but is now confirming.

Scripture teaches that imitation is a reliable educator. As has been noted above, Paul urges imitation in his epistles. Paul is not alone in this, as two other apostles and writers of the New Testament, the apostles Peter and John, emphasize the need for imitation: "For what credit is it if, when you sin and are beaten for it, you endure? But if when you do good and suffer for it you endure, this is a gracious thing in the sight of God. For to this you have been called, because Christ also suffered for you, leaving you an example, so that you might follow in his steps" (1 Pet 2:20–21); "Beloved, do not imitate what is evil but imitate good. Whoever does good is from God; whoever does evil has not seen God" (3 John 1:11). Most significantly, Jesus relied on it. As he washes the feet of his disciples, he says, "For I have given you an example, that you also should do just as I have done to you" (John 13:15).

Emulation requires an exemplar, a model, one who can provide a pattern to imitate. In his epistle to the Romans, the apostle Paul explicitly refers

---

48. Chrysostom, "Address on Vainglory," 117.
49. Chrysostom, "Address on Vainglory," 117.
50. Chrysostom, "Address on Vainglory," 117.
51. For further study, see Chrysostom and Malingrey, *Sur la vaine gloire*, 180.

to the jealousy provoked by emulation or imitation as a means to induce his listeners to follow his model. "If by any means I may provoke to emulation [*parazēlōsō*] *them which are* my flesh, and might save some of them" (Rom 11:14 KJV). Paul sees this jealousy, or zeal, that provokes imitation as something that can be used in either a positive or negative way. In this statement, he shows that this envy (to be like another) can actually be used to lead a person to salvation. Chrysostom also desires to use imitation as a means to Christlikeness. He echoes Paul when he urges parents to point out good companions for their children to imitate. He also would have his listeners harness this natural ability as a learning device.

Furthermore, Chrysostom emphatically underscores the need for parents to live a life of holiness, to be the pattern of living for their children's sake. He gives specific biblical examples to imitate: "Why, tell me, do ye not imitate them of old? Tell me! You women, especially, emulate those admirable women. Has a child been born to anyone? Imitate Hannah's example [1 Sam 1:24]; look at what she did . . . she was absorbed in one object, how from the very beginning she might dedicate the spiritual image to God."[52] Parents are to imitate their spiritual templates as their children imitate them in turn.

Chrysostom was asking the parents in his congregation to harness a natural ability with intent. The old "do as I say, not as I do," would not work. He understood the young would imitate their parents, even if the parents did not intentionally realize or wish to be imitated. The unintentional, thoughtless example set by the parent is absorbed by the child just as easily as the intentional, thoughtful one. The careless pattern will be followed as surely as the lovely one. So, if this is the case, the parent needs to make the effort to repeatedly live righteously, in terms of the Christian life, until this way of life is so much a part of who she has become that she will be a good example to her children, whether or not she is thinking about it. Will Durant's interpretation of Aristotle was right, in this sense, when he said, "We are what we repeatedly do. Excellence, then, is not an act, but a habit."[53] The only qualifier that a church father like Chrysostom would add is that this habit of virtue is not attainable outside of the church and the divine energy of God at work in the heart.

To further emphasize the correctness of Chrysostom's insistence on imitation and the right kind of models, contemporary Christians have the benefit of current scientific advances in this area. In his editorial introduction

---

52. Chrysostom, "Homily 21," in *Homilies on Ephesians*, 154.
53. Durant, *Story of Philosophy*, 69.

to *Mimesis and Science,* psychologist Scott Garrels wrote this, describing the impact of the last fifty years of research on imitation:

> Far from being the simple and mindless act that we typically associate it with ("monkey see, monkey do"), imitation is now understood as a complex, generative, and multidimensional phenomenon at the heart of what makes us human . . . . Researchers now argue that imitation is an innate, and characteristically human, ability that guides cognitive and social development from the very beginning of life, both from developmental and evolutionary perspectives . . . . In fact, so foundational is our capacity to imitate, that many researchers believe it to be the linchpin that contributed to a wide-scale neural reorganization of the brain, allowing for the coevolution of more complex social, cultural and representational abilities from earlier primates to humans.[54]

Dr. Andrew Meltzoff of the University of Washington's Institute for Learning and Brain Sciences was one of the scientists who demonstrated that the first act of newborns is to imitate, sometimes as early as the first hour of birth. This completely contradicted the previous belief that infants were asocial isolates who lacked the ability to connect with others. "*Humans imitate before they can use language; they learn through imitation but don't need to learn to imitate.*"[55]

What neuroscientists and developmental psychologists are discovering today about the innate ability to learn through imitation would come as no surprise to Chrysostom, Jesus, or any of the other biblical teachers and prophets. These ancients understood that human beings are social creatures who need a community to learn and thrive, who would whither like a tree deprived of sunlight and water without others to help them grow. This is exactly what human experience has shown to be true, as abandoned children who grow in the wild without human contact suffer fates much worse than those depicted in *The Jungle Book* or *Tarzan*. These feral children, once discovered, are found to lack the basic means of communication, their mental development is retarded, their physical state malnourished.

What Chrysostom also knew about children and the human ability to learn is that examples to imitate do not necessarily need to be alive or even real people. In the next section, I show how intimately related imitation and story-telling are in his pedagogy.

---

54. Garrels, "Human Imitation," 1, 3.
55. Meltzoff, "Out of the Mouths," 59.

STEP THREE: STORY-TELLING

In Chrysostom's psychology of the five basic senses, it becomes clear that story-telling is interconnected fundamentally with the first two elements described in the previous sections. The inner mind of the child is fed by stories, and this "food" either starves or nourishes the fruits of *askesis* and imitation. Thus, Chrysostom saw a way to "exploit to the full that love for stories which is characteristic of all normal children."[56] What the youth watches and hears especially affects his moral outlook. Chrysostom instructs parents not to let their children listen to gossip, idle talk, or old-wives' tales, but instead be fed the great stories of the Bible. Chrysostom was not shy in pointing out which biblical figures children could use as models. Indeed, Laistner noted that, "His familiarity with the Bible and his vast store of *exempla* were never diminished."[57]

In "On Vainglory," Chrysostom uses two narratives from the Hebrew Scriptures to teach parents the way they should tell stories. He begins, "Once upon a time there were two sons of one father, even two brothers.... The elder was a tiller of the ground, the younger a shepherd" (Gen 4:1–16). As he proceeds, he pauses to point out how parents can slowly introduce concepts, such as envy, even to the very young, as the story is told repeatedly over time. St. John also recommends how much the parent should relate in the stories and urges them to wait to tell scenes of explicit violence, recommending the use of simple language and age appropriateness in saving certain stories for the child when he grew older.

Yet story-time still needs to be fun and engaging. He advises, "Make thy stories agreeable that they may give the child pleasure and his soul may not grow weary."[58] This is why story-telling and imitation are interconnected. How to act and be are provided through models nearest to the young. Through stories of saints and heroes, children are given a wealth of exemplars. Some of these models are fictional or legendary, like those provided in fables. Of course, those closest to the child have a greater impact, but fictional and historical exemplars could also be powerful models. Like Athanasius, Chrysostom believed that it is the community in which the child is reared that will enable or prevent the attainment of virtue, and it will do so with the shared treasury of its stories, along with the elders and mentors provided by such a community.

---

56. Laistner, *Christianity and Pagan Culture*, 35.
57. Laistner, *Christianity and Pagan Culture*, 84.
58. Laistner, *Christianity and Pagan Culture*, 102.

Story-telling through drama is also to be used, but cautiously. "Never send thy son to the theater that he may not suffer utter corruption through his ears and eyes."[59] In an era where televised violence, profanity, and promiscuity are common, and the question of whether exposure to these forms of media is harmful is debated, there is no doubt to Chrysostom's view on the question. Guarding the senses also guards the heart, which is "the seat and habitation of spirit."[60] Like the athlete who must abstain from certain kinds of food, or the city whose militia must protect against marauders, the child must be shielded from that which harmfully assails the senses. It is the Christian parent, as the child's foremost guide and mentor, who must discriminate wisely between harmful and helpful, the good fruit that can be tasted and provide nourishment, and the bad that would poison.

Chrysostom had more advice for parents. If a parent went so far as to not allow the child to see a popular play, he considered it a good thing, but Chrysostom urged these parents to compensate their child in other ways, saying, "Let us devise for him other harmless pleasures . . . let us give him recreation, let us show our regard for him by many gifts, so that his soul may patiently bear our rejection of the theatre."[61] This advice might seem funny, but if one thinks about the anger of a preteen who is denied the latest Tarentino movie or the remake of another Stephen King adaptation to film that all of his friends have seen, we might seriously consider his words.

As parents exhibit a pattern of Christlikeness to follow and offer vicarious models in stories and Scripture readings, Chrysostom has this encouragement to give:

> "For," says He, "*seek first His kingdom, and all these things shall be added to you*" [Matt 6:33]. What sort of persons, think you, must the children of such parents will be? What the servants of such masters? What all others who come near them? Will not they too eventually be loaded with blessings out of number? For generally the servants also have their characters formed after their master's, and are fashioned after their humors, love the same objects, speak the same language, and engage in them in the same pursuits. If we thus regulate ourselves, and attentively study the Scriptures, in most things we shall derive instruction from them.[62]

---

59. Chrysostom, "Address on Vainglory," 56.
60. Chrysostom, "Address on Vainglory," 112.
61. Chrysostom, "Address on Vainglory," 117–18.
62. Chrysostom, "Homily 20," in *Homilies on Ephesians*, 152.

A HOLISTIC MORAL EDUCATION

After examining all three pillars of Chrysostom's pedagogy, it is time to stand back and look at the edifice created. The following chapters will make a case for why these three pillars, built upon the foundation of the theanthropic ethic, come together to make a moral and spiritual education that befits the family as the little church.

Other contemporary thinkers have examined how the first two pillars—*askesis* and positive *mimesis*—build from one another, so a brief review is in order. Brian Robinette makes a convincing argument that positive *mimesis* is possible only through *askesis* and that the desert fathers deserve further consideration on creative mutuality.[63] Robinette explores the connection between *askesis* and *mimesis* through the writings of two desert fathers, Evagrius Ponticus and St. John Cassian. Evagrius in particular will be discussed in the following two chapters with this concept in mind.

Robinette draws from the research of Jean-Michel Oughourlian, psychologist and long-time collaborator with René Girard. Oughourlian believes that the only possible way to sustain positive relationships with others is through "day-to-day asceticism."[64] Oughourlian is not counselling a community of monks but couples in committed relationships. He sees *askesis* as the necessary generator of positive *mimesis*. With this argument in mind, Robinette turns to Evagrius and Cassian for supporting evidence. He believes the desert fathers of the fourth and fifth centuries had a "profound intuitive grasp" of what is known today as mimetic theory and that the ascetical-contemplative practices developed by the desert monastics effectually combatted acquisitive (negative) mimetic desire and instead cultivated positive *mimesis*.[65] According to mimetic theory, authentic selfhood is gained only through positive reciprocation, "premised upon the attitudinal and behavioral hospitality to the otherness that founds it."[66] This is contrasted with acquisitive *mimesis*, where one harbors the illusion of absolute difference between herself and her neighbor. This illusion pushes the self to desire freedom *from* the other, locking the individual into a pattern of distorted and antagonistic behavior with her neighbor.

Returning to the idea of authentic selfhood and hospitality, Robinette notes that the goal of desert monasticism was not so much a flight away from others but, instead, toward the other, with the end goal being love.

---

63. See Robinette, "Deceit, Desire."
64. Oughourlian, as quoted in Robinette, "Deceit, Desire," 130.
65. Robinette, "Deceit, Desire," 131.
66. Robinette, "Deceit, Desire," 134.

In other words, it was a spiritual training ground meant to teach the disciple how to love his neighbor. "The goal of the ascetic life is charity," writes Evagrius, and both he and Cassian agree that disinterested love, love unmotivated by fear or reward, is the fruit of *apatheia*.[67] The spiritual exercises of attention, discernment, and abnegation all have the love of neighbor and God as their ultimate goal. Rowan Williams states the idea concisely: "You 'flee' to the desert not to escape neighbors but to grasp more fully what the neighbor is . . ."[68]

Thus, Cassian describes a kind of reformation that the disciple must undergo, which amounts to a reformation of the mimetic capacity. The reformation happens through the "skillful imitation" of the spiritual elders in the community, which is coupled with contemplative practices that train the disciple to understand God "alone as the source and of all pacific desire."[69] Evagrius and Cassian both view *askesis* as a tradition passed down from Jesus Christ to his followers, as a "living chain" that transfigures the disciple into the image of her Master. This "skillful imitation," through daily *askesis* in community with the neighbor, is eschatological, as it both realizes and anticipates the kingdom of God.

Although John Cassian and Evagrius were writing to novice monastics, Chrysostom was clear in his preaching to the Christians of Antioch and Constantinople that no follower of Christ was exempt from "day-to-day asceticism." He knew how difficult it would be for the disciples who did not "flee to the desert" but instead married, had children, and lived lives among non-followers of Christ. Christian parents are not immune to worries, fears, fatigue, and material concerns. Exercises in prayer and contemplation, and the imitation of good models, become much harder with the distractions of life and the ever-present temptation to follow in the footsteps of the materially successful. Yet, like Oughourlian, Chrysostom believed it was not only possible but necessary. The kingdom must be sought, no matter what circumstances life presents, if one is truly a follower of Jesus Christ.

If Robinette is right, then *askesis* must be practiced in order to truly nurture positive *mimesis* and not see the neighbor as a constant rival or obstacle to overcome. In a consumer culture where greed is considered good and "friendly" competition harmless, this concept seems counterintuitive. Yet Christianity is counter to the wisdom of the world, which makes Robinette's argument, as well as Oughourlian's and Chrysostom's, plausible.

---

67. Evagrius, as quoted in Robinette, "Deceit, Desire," 135.
68. Rowan Williams, as quoted in Robinette, "Deceit, Desire," 136.
69. Robinette, "Deceit, Desire," 136.

So, two of the pillars interconnect, but does story-telling fit equally? As will be argued in chapter 5, the nature of story-telling reveals its ability to change the mental landscape of the listener or reader. The mimetic capacity, which allows for empathy, works within the world of the imaginary as well. Thus, the vicarious nature of the story not only allows for the vicarious practice of virtue (the cultivation of virtue being the second fruit of *askesis*) but for the imitation of an external mediator. For the interior world of the mind, story-telling has the potential to allow for *askesis* and always offers a model to imitate through the character. As being a steady model of Christlikeness is difficult for Christian parents in differing stages of spiritual maturity, story-telling becomes a useful aid to the parent, providing an abundance of models that reinforce the right way of life.

Whether the story does the first and whether the model is good or bad, all depends on the story told. Therefore, Chrysostom is clear that the child of a Christian household should not be exposed to gossip, vicious or gratuitous stories, or the theater (being both vicious *and* gratuitous in sex and violence). He knew the power of the story, which is why he encouraged the telling and retelling of Bible stories or any that had Christian themes. It was ultimately up to the parents to use discernment (cultivated through *askesis*) to know what stories to tell their children. If the parents did not have this discernment, they were to seek the advice of a spiritual mentor.

In this way, all three pillars are interconnected, flowing from *askesis*, to positive *mimesis*, to story-telling, all nourishing and cultivating each other. When practiced as a family, the family indeed becomes the little church, as the Holy Spirit, named the Treasury of good things and the Giver of life, works in and through its members.

SUMMARY

Chrysostom's guide to bringing children into the life of Christ might seem too simple, calling only for *askesis*, imitation, and story-telling. However, simple does not mean *easy*. St. John is calling for a higher standard for Christians than their fellow peers in the secular world, as well as a harder road to follow than that of the celibate who has devoted herself to a life of solitary struggle. Tackling the passions through *askesis* is impossible without God's divine work in the life of the one who attempts this, just as the attainment and habituation of virtue requires complete cooperation with the Holy Spirit. The temptation to vainglory might be the preeminent obstacle to the parent, but it is accompanied by a plethora of other temptations and demons.

Likewise, being a model of Christ to one's family is no easy task, possible only through the slow habituation of Christian virtue by the practice of the spiritual disciplines. Story-telling, compared to the first two elements, is perhaps the least difficult for the parents to accomplish, if they are willing to carve out the necessary time from lives filled with busyness.

Finally, it is good to remember that Chrysostom's "little church" is meant to be embedded in the greater church—the fellowship of life that is the body of Christ. None of what Chrysostom recommends or instructs is possible external to the faith community. The parent, too, needs mentoring, and those mentors can be found only in the church. These are the elders and deacons, ministers and widows who have the spiritual maturation to act as guides to the next generation. He imagines a youth trained up, finally grown, and marrying, about to start a little church of his own: "If we lead him to the bridal chamber with a training such as this, consider how great a gift he will be to the bride . . . let us invite Christ there, for the bridegroom is worthy of Him. Let us invite His disciples; all things shall be of the best for the groom. And he himself will learn to train his own sons in this way, and they theirs in turn, and the result will be a golden cord."[70]

The next chapter focuses on the first of Chrysostom's three elements, *askesis*. In this discussion of spiritual discipline, I explain the patristic theology-ethic of *askesis* as Chrysostom knew it based on the teachings of the day, its relationship to spiritual formation, the passions, *apatheia*, and three different types of exercises discussed by Chrysostom in "On Vainglory." My in-depth examination of the first pillar of Chrysostom's moral formation will hopefully give parents a sense of clarity, as well as urgency, concerning this aspect of their child's upbringing and show how Christian spirituality is never truly separate from Christian morality and virtue.

70. Chrysostom, "Address on Vainglory," 121–22.

3

Becoming Real

Askesis *and Spiritual Formation*

HERE BEGINS THE STUDY of the first element of Chrysostom's "golden cord." It is natural to start with *askesis*, as without the self-control cultivated by spiritual practice, there is no foundation for resisting the second element (*mimesis*) in its negative form, and no spiritual acuity or instinct for the third element (story-telling). In chapter 2, I introduced *askesis* and explained that to St. John Chrysostom the life of spiritual discipline was not the sole domain of the monastic but was instead the major obligation of *every* Christian. Chrysostom felt the need to remind the families of his congregation of this truth, that spiritual exercise is a basic part of the Christian life, not something set apart for a small segment of "special" people within the church. It was so important to him that he spent a good part of his time speaking on ascetical practices in "On Vainglory."

Given its importance, the following pages will reveal *askesis* as the spiritual battleground where the Christian disciple wars with the "passions" of the old self, that she might leave behind the slave's mentality and grasp the freedom that was bestowed on the cross of Christ. Without *askesis*, there is no freedom to cultivate Christian fruit. This is the starting point of spiritual formation, of cooperation with the Holy Spirit in becoming like the second Adam. As spiritual formation is a fundamental part of the Christian life, Chrysostom believed that it was imperative that Christian parents take responsibility not only for their own spiritual lives but for the spiritual development of their children. I follow his lead, first by examining the premodern theology-ethic of *askesis* as Chrysostom would have understood it, its relationship to *theosis*, the passions, *apatheia*, and finally, the different kinds of spiritual exercises he encouraged.

ST. JOHN'S THEOLOGY AS A BASIS FOR THE ASCETICAL LIFE

I was once asked if St. John's theology really mattered to contemporary parents. After all, most Christian parents today are not familiar with patristic theology and do not attend churches that are based on its teachings. The implication behind the question was that parents do not care about or need theory and theology; they just needed the practical know-how or advice that I could glean from Chrysostom's teaching.

As a parent, I respectfully disagree with this attitude. John's theological background matters because it affects *how* he viewed spiritual formation. Theory precedes method. I cannot know (or explain) why John prescribes a certain method without understanding the theology that precedes his thinking. Christian parents interested in receiving his moral instruction, even if it is reconceived in contemporary terms, should know the reasons behind John's affirmation of *askesis* in teaching the young. If we as Christian parents truly want to see the spiritual maturity of our entire families increase, working through John's theology is at the very least a thought-provoking exercise. Even if parents disagree with certain points in his theology, they still benefit by the introspection it inspires concerning their spiritual development.

Chrysostom's belief in the deep connection between *askesis* and sanctification, and his resolution that the Christian household is a "little church," are a result of his premodern Christian theology. His view of *askesis* cannot be understood apart from the theology he was grounded in, the patristic theology of Late Antiquity. Before entering into a discussion of the kinds of spiritual disciplines he promoted for the moral growth of Christian families, it is necessary to understand Chrysostom's theological context. As emphasized in chapter 2, I argue for the historical retrieval of his thought on moral education. There is value in having a theological guide at this point, as we cannot assume his embedded theology is the same as ours. Presuming it is causes confusion and misunderstanding. Likewise, not only his theology but his ethic should be made clear, as premodern Christianity did not differentiate between the two. Chrysostom's theology is his ethic, and his ethic is his theology, and in order to understand his practical and pastoral guidance for parents, he has to be placed within his theological context.

Therefore, I seek to delve to the root of Chrysostom's method for moral education by exploring the theology that is its foundation. What is key in understanding this theology-ethic, which is the source of his pedagogy, is that it is not separate from his spirituality. In other words, this moral education is also spiritual formation, thereby making it deeply theological in nature. Note again the coupling of theology, ethics, and spirituality. This is in stark contrast with post-Enlightenment intellectual practice, which divides these areas of thought with knife-edge precision, placing them into separate categories.

With this in mind, I approach the first element of Chrysostom's educational framework. *Askesis* is spiritual exercise or practice. Spiritual practice is guided by theological and biblical teaching and has a profound purpose: *spiritual transformation*. The family, in its ideal form as a little church, seeks Christlikeness together, practices spiritual-moral formation together, and is transformed by the grace of the Holy Spirit together. So the "little church" is patterned after and included within the big church, which seeks the transformation of its members into little Christs for the salvation of the world.

A helpful way to think about Chrysostom's concept of spiritual formation is through allegory. Big concepts, he knew, are made palatable through stories. Carlo Collodi's *Pinocchio* is just such a story. It is a tale about a transformation. *Pinocchio* is a fairy tale that begins with a magical piece of wood. This magic wood, in the hands of a skilled craftsmen, is shaped and carved into the likeness of a boy. The puppet has many misadventures as he learns how to love his creator as his father, learns the difference between foolishness and wisdom, and learns to listen to the good spirits that guide instead of the bad company that surrounds him.

All these lessons are in pursuit of becoming a *real* boy and a real son to his father. Pinocchio is a children's story, but as a metaphor it fits Chrysostom's theology of sanctification. Every Christian, every "little Christ," is called to become "real." Jesus Christ is the perfect template for real humanity, and the more the disciple grows into his likeness, the more real she becomes. Think for a moment about the brief introduction to the theanthropic ethic in chapter 1. This is the ethic of *theosis*. Humanity is to become like God. Therefore, the first part of this discussion of St. John's theology of *askesis* will begin with the doctrines that pertain to God.

I begin with how Chrysostom and his contemporaries conceived of the good in relationship to God. When delving into the arena of moral realism, the conversation usually starts with a description or definition of what is meant by good(s). Moral terms can be fungible, and it is important to determine what Chrysostom means when he uses terms like good, bad, evil, right, fit, etc. To Chrysostom, God is the foundation of moral realism, as he *is* the Good and the Source of the good. Every understanding of good, law, pleasure, perfection, value, love, and so on is part of the totality that is the goodness of God. Indeed, God is above all good and all that can be conceived of as good. This understanding underlies Chrysostom's theology-ethic and especially his understanding of how God relates to humanity. The only way he can answer any question regarding "the good" is to begin with a theology of God. Therefore, the following discussion tackles the key doctrines that form the basis for Chrysostom's understanding of *askesis*. These doctrines include (1) the apophatic way of knowing God and how this affects spiritual practice, (2) the doctrine of the Trinity as a basis for *askesis*, and (3) the doctrine of the incarnation.

The Apophatic Attitude as a Posture for Spiritual Practice

Chrysostom would have had some theological training in apophatic theology.[1] In attempting to understand his view of *askesis*, it is helpful to know what apophaticism is and how it might affect spiritual practice. Although modern Christian parents might never approach theology using this method, the following discussion will look at apophaticism in terms of posture or attitude and how apophaticism as an attitude can facilitate ascetical practice.

According to the *Areopagitica*, there are two paths the disciple can take to learn about God. The first is through positive theology, or *cataphatic* theology, which moves toward an understanding of God through affirmations. This first way was believed to lead to some knowledge of God but is possibly hindered by misplaced trust in the human being's power of reason. Gregory of Nyssa saw cataphatic theology as a slippery slope into idolatry, as "every concept relative to God is a simulacrum, a false likeness, an idol."[2] Any idea of God that the human mind could conceive might actually be an unintended idol of the human imagination instead of the true reality of God.

Gregory of Nyssa agreed with Pseudo Dionysius in his assessment that apophatic theology was the best means to knowing God. Since knowledge is based on what is, i.e., scientific knowledge is based on scientific facts, the question arises on how one can truly know anything about the Uncreated Being who is beyond *all* that exists. God is, therefore, first and

---

1. Apophaticism uses negations to form an understanding of God, while cataphatic, or positive, theology uses affirmations. However, even the affirmations of positive theology are apophatic in nature, as God is described as limit*less*, *un*searchable, *im*mutable, *im*mortal, *in*finite, etc.

2. Lossky, *Mystical Theology*, 33.

foremost, to be understood as unknowable, and the first step to approaching him is humility.

Humility is the foremost virtue in thinking apophatically, because it means acknowledging, as created beings, utter ignorance. Yet it is in the paradoxical unknowing, this admitted ignorance, that God allows the frail and ignorant human being to draw near. It is because of this use of apophatic theology, approaching God through the darkness of ignorance like Moses climbing up a mist-enshrouded Sinai, that this theology is rightly called mystic. To approach God is an ascent, and it begins from the lowest place of humility and ignorance. "Come, and let us go up to the mountain of the Lord, to the house of the God of Jacob; He will teach us His ways, and we shall walk in His paths" (Isa 2:3 NKJV). The seeker of God ascends to him, moves to him, leans in toward him. This is the posture of the life in Christ, movement toward God. The one who approaches must leave everything he thinks he knows behind, remove his sandals, and dare to approach God where he is.

One way to grasp apophaticism is to see it in action. When I was a graduate student in divinity school, one of the theology professors, an internationally recognized professor from South Korea, always removed her shoes before stepping into her classroom to teach. To even speak concerning the things of God, to speak of the sacred, demands humility. Her response to her life's work as a teacher was one of humility and respect toward God.

Apophaticism, as a theological approach, affects Chrysostom's theology-ethic because of the attitude it demands the disciple to adopt when practicing the spiritual disciplines. Apophaticism, although not the preferred method of theology in contemporary Western Christianity, is useful in at least reminding the practitioner of "day-to-day asceticism," that to approach God calls for the humbling of the self. For if knowing God is possible only by approaching him, then the one who approaches must go through a fundamental transition, from one kind of human being to another. This is the purpose of *askesis* and the definition of sanctification. Moses was changed during the forty days on the mountain, so much so that when he descended the mountain to his people, they were afraid to look at his face. He veiled himself from that moment forward, to hide his transformation (Exod 34:28–35). Chrysostom's spiritual formation becomes apophatic theology in action. The transformation into Christ, to bear his likeness, is a theological act.

Note that one aspect of apophaticism is its emphasis of experience over reason. Yet it is "not necessarily a theology of ecstasy." Instead, it is a disposition, or "an attitude of the mind which refuses to form concepts about God." Theologian Vladimir Lossky better explains:

Such an attitude utterly excludes all abstract and purely intellectual theology which would adapt the mysteries of the wisdom of God to human ways of thought. It is an existential attitude which involves the whole man: there is no theology apart from experience; it is necessary to change, to become a new man. To know God one must draw near to Him . . . . Apophaticism is, therefore, a criterion: the sure sign of an attitude of mind conformed to truth. In this sense all true theology is fundamentally apophatic.[3]

As Lossky states, it is better to think of this as simply an attitude to adopt when praying, fasting, etc. As the disciple draws nearer to God, starting from a place of humility and ignorance, he bears the correct disposition needed for *askesis*. As he approaches God through self-emptiness, he can come to know God. But the knowing is relational. To be drawn to the unknowable God is to be drawn to the Trinity. The goal of apophatic theology is relationship with God.

The Doctrine of the Trinity as a Basis for Askesis

This next section will explain how Chrysostom understood the Trinity. When speaking of theology as relational, or of God being relational, we are actually speaking about God's personal, Trinitarian nature. In the preceding paragraphs, I explained that the early fathers, including Chrysostom, believed that God is the *Source* of good and *is* the Good. Yet if *askesis*, combined with an attitude of humility and ignorance, draws us into a relationship with the Uncreated Being, what does this mean in terms of God in Trinity? To Chrysostom and other early Christian thinkers, God in Trinity is not only ultimate reality but also is where good exists essentially.[4] The human being can know good only insofar as she knows God in Trinity. God's very existence as Trinity reveals that the source of the Good is *interpersonal relatedness*.

God's relational nature means that to know the Good is to know the divine Persons in communion with one another. In speaking of the consubstantiality of the Three, the premodern fathers used what were once synonymous words, *ousia* (meaning individual substance) and *hypostasis* (existence or subsistence) and forever changed them to mean the difference

---

3. Lossky, *Mystical Theology*, 38–39.
4. Gregory Nazianzen, through his theological poetry, provides examples of patristic thinking on the Trinity.

between what is common (God in One *Substance*) and the particular (and Three *Persons*).

Chrysostom's theology insists on a certain attitude (apophatic) that the Bible phrases as "fear of the Lord" (Prov 9:10; Prov 10:27; Isa 11:2; Acts 9:31), and Chrysostom saw *askesis* as the means to freedom, a freedom that allows the Christian disciple to know God as a Person. In speaking on the meaning of "person," contemporary Christian philosopher Christos Yannaras speaks of God's revelation of himself as "the personal hypostasis of eternal life." As the ultimate reality and the ultimate personal existence, distinctive and free, God answers Moses, "I am he who is" (Exod 3:14).

God reveals himself in history as the God of Abraham, Isaac, and Jacob, a real Person who speaks with real people. Since God in Trinity is ultimate reality and the ethical source for humankind, then ethical and moral activity of the human being is also accomplished in *community* and never as isolated individuals, just as God is eternally in community. This is important, as this concept of God also shapes the concept of divine love. "It is the Father who distinguishes the hypostases 'in an eternal movement of love.'"[5]

To summarize, the apophatic attitude acknowledges that no human concept of God is perfect. God transcends all human notions of good, nature, and persons. God in Trinity is beyond all these things. To know God, then, is possible only relationally. God allows himself to be known through his Personhood.

The apophatic attitude is necessary in approaching the personal God through *askesis*. There is another aspect to this attitude to mention. Along with humility and ignorance, the church fathers, including Chrysostom, speak of repentance (*metanoia*). Returning to their teaching on the Trinity will show the connection between the correct mindset for *askesis* and God as three Persons. Gregory Nazianzen writes: "No sooner do I conceive of the One than I am illumined by the splendor of the Three; no sooner do I distinguish them than I am carried back to the One. When I think of any One of the Three, I think of Him as the whole, and my eyes are filled, and the greater part of what I am thinking escapes me . . . . When I contemplate the Three together, I see but one torch, and cannot divide or measure out the undivided light."[6]

God is not bound or defined by any multiplicity. God "transcends all separation."[7] Basil expresses this idea:

---

5. Lossky, *Mystical Theology*, 60.
6. Gregory Nazianzen, as quoted in Lossky, *Mystical Theology*, 46.
7. Lossky, *Mystical Theology*, 47.

> We do not count by addition, passing from the one to the many
> by increase; we do not say: one, two, three, or first, second and
> third. *"For I am God, the first, and I am the last."* Now we have
> never, even to the present time, heard of a second God; but
> adoring God of God, confessing the individuality of the hypos-
> tases, we dwell in the monarchy without dividing the theology
> into fragments.[8]

The sum might always be 3=1, but God in Trinity is not a quantity but instead "an indivisible united divine hypostases."[9] Trinity reveals both God's perfection and plenitude. It is the Triune God, who is infinite, unchangeable, and inscrutable, to whom the human being can draw near only through grace and only through *metanoia*, the utter change of spirit seen in Job who says, "I had heard of you by the hearing of the ear, but now my eye sees you; therefore I despise myself, and repent in dust and ashes" (Job 42:5–6).

The theology of the Trinity is what Chrysostom's theology-ethic hinges upon, as it is a theology of fullness and union. Everyone, as Job, must repent in "dust and ashes" and change in spirit, becoming a new human, in order to, as the apostle says, "become partakers of the divine nature."[10] Yet how can this promise be possible when the created human being is so substantially different than that of the Uncreated Being, who is beyond all nature as well as all limitations, finitude, and goodness? What by nature is impossible for the created being becomes possible through *grace*.

For this reason, Jesus upholds the publican instead of the Pharisee as the model to follow (Luke 18:9–14). The Pharisee, as the religious man, seeks his own salvation, through his own individual moral capacities and achievements of virtue and in abiding by the law. Yet Jesus rejects him in favor of those who, in humility, surrender themselves to God's mercy and love: the publican, the thief, the prostitute, the prodigal, and all those who "embody the repentance, the radical change in mentality and way of thinking, the understanding of life as relationship and of death as individual self-sufficiency."[11] Therefore, Chrysostom believed that the correct attitude of *askesis* was a mentality of humility, ignorance, and repentance.

As seen so far in patristic teaching on the Trinity, Chrysostom viewed God as both inaccessible and accessible, approachable and unapproachable, communicable and incommunicable. If the apophatic attitude (humility, ignorance, repentance) is meant to draw the disciple nearer to God through

---

8. Lossky, *Mystical Theology*, 47–48.
9. Lossky, *Mystical Theology*, 47–48.
10. "γένησθε θείας κοινωνοὶ φύσεως" (2 Pet 1:4, in Nestle, *Bible*).
11. Yannaras, *Meaning of Reality*, 176–77.

askesis, this teaching makes this goal seem downright impossible. Yet there is another patristic doctrine that speaks to this paradox. It is the doctrine of the uncreated *energies* of God, distinct from God's essence, yet wholly and indivisibly God. "It is by His energies that we say we know our God; we do not assert that we can come near to the essence itself, for His energies descend to us, but His essence remains unapproachable."[12]

These energies described by the church fathers are sometimes referred to as "operations," "actions," or "works" of God, connoting a mode of existence that manifests his self throughout the universe. Other times, the word energy is simply called "grace," "uncreated light," or "the glory of God." Indeed, Divine Love, or "love-energy," is simply grace. Whatever name given, the energy of God is placed within both the theology of the Trinity and the doctrine of the divine economy of God. It is God's presence in these outpourings of light to which humankind is beckoned to approach. "The glory of God appears to those who love Him, the righteous, in the Hebrew Scripture. "God cometh from Teman, and the Holy One from Mount Paran. His glory covereth the heavens, and the earth is full of His praise. And a brightness appeareth as the light; rays hath He at His side; and there is the hiding of His power" (Hab 3:3–4 JPS Tanakh 1917). In the New Testament Scriptures, Jesus' divinity is made manifest on the mountain during the transfiguration (Matt 17:2; Mark 9:2; Luke 9:29). The glory of God, revealed to the cosmos throughout time, is reality and must be understood realistically.

In light of this teaching, the follower of Christ, including the Christian family, is to participate in the kingdom of God, in union with God, and this happens through God's grace, the grace of countless names. It is through his energy that the inaccessible Trinity can be made known to the world, as God is both the One "who dwells in unapproachable light, whom no one has ever seen or can see" (1 Tim 6:16) and yet the One of whom his Son can promise, "If anyone loves Me, he will keep My word; and My Father will love him, and We will come to him and make Our abode with him" (John 14:23 NASB). This theology of grace promises that even the human being, who is created and finite and is substantially *not* God, can still receive the promise, that by grace, not by nature, she can dwell in the house of the Lord and take a seat at the wedding banquet (Luke 14:15–24). As Lossky says succinctly, "We remain creatures while becoming God by grace, as Christ remained God in becoming man by the Incarnation."[13]

---

12. Chrysostom, as quoted in Lossky in *Mystical Theology*, 72.

13. Lossky, *Mystical Theology*, 87.

The Doctrine of the Incarnation as a Basis for Askesis

In the next several paragraphs I focus on Chrysostom's view of the Second Person of the Trinity and, moreover, how he would have understood the incarnation in connection with *askesis*. It is by reason of the incarnation that his theology-ethic can be called *theanthropic*, for as the Second Person of the Trinity emptied himself and descended into this world, assuming a fully human nature, he became the "theanthropos." The following explanation by St. Maximus the Confessor helps to make sense of Chrysostom's economy of the Son: "The finite and the infinite—things which exclude one another and cannot be mixed—are found to be united in Him and are manifested mutually in one and the other."[14] The concept of *kenosis*, the self-abandonment or self-emptying of the Second Person, reveals the Son in his greatest manifestation. His two natures paradoxically remain "distinct and unmixed" but permeate one another, without being transformed into one another, in perichoresis.

Chrysostom's theological understanding of Jesus, the Second Person, as the incarnation is of great importance to his view of salvation. As will be discussed more fully in the next chapter, Eastern Christian teaching holds that it was sin of the will that placed all of humanity into a "new existential mode of being," the state of sin and mortality, a state that is as close as creation can get to "non-being."[15] In this discussion of *askesis*, it must be remarked that this new state put three obstacles in the way of humanity, preventing all from reaching their God-given *telos*. These three barriers were sin, death, and nature. The divine plan for Adam, which would have been a straight ascent to God, was upended by Adam's choice of radical (and false) autonomy and self-sufficiency. The path to God was now confused and barricaded by these three impassable obstacles.

The early church fathers taught that what humanity needed was the removal of these obstacles or, in other words, salvation. God therefore made the way to himself passable again, by inverting the path of ascent—now blocked by sin, death, and nature—and *descending* to his creatures. In reverse order, he removed each barrier: the last first, that of *nature*, by the incarnation; the second, *sin*, through his death on the cross; the third, *death*, through his resurrection. As Maximus taught, the incarnation and deification imply one another, as God descends into the world to become human, and the human being is raised to divine plenitude through grace. In this way, Jesus Christ, as the second Adam, successfully fulfils the *telos* that the first Adam was given and did not complete.

---

14. Maximus, as quoted in Lossky, *Mystical Theology*, 142.
15. Lossky, *Mystical Theology*, 135.

God, in giving the freedom of morality to his creature, the human being, foreknew the failure of Adam before time began, yet his *telos* for creation never changed. Jesus Christ voluntarily assumed human nature, condescending to enter the fallen world that was corrupted by sin and death, in order to resolve the terrible dilemma caused by the sinful will of humanity. In the form of the incarnation, God created a bridge to humanity, a bridge from death to salvation. Chrysostom and other church fathers saw relationship with Jesus Christ, by way of grace, as the road to salvation.

It is the incarnation, the knowledge that the Second Person of the Trinity "assumed a full human nature in time," that makes it possible to understand Chrysostom's view of the human *telos*.[16] Chrysostom also understood that this salvation made the human being *entirely whole*. The incarnation speaks to the reality that the spiritual growth of the believer toward participation with God is *not* simply or completely a spiritual reality. The sanctification of the *body* as well as the spirit is promised, and this "psychosomatic reality" mirrors the unity of the two natures in Jesus Christ. This promised reality is eschatological in that it will be fulfilled completely only at the time of the resurrection in the last days, when "the dead will be raised imperishable, and we shall be changed" (1 Cor 15:52).

Another concern for Chrysostom's theology of the incarnation has to do with the physical nature and what is good and natural as opposed to what is sinful and unnatural. The physical body, the *soma*, was created by God and is good.[17] When Scripture speaks of the body in the negative, it is referring to *sarx*, or the sinful and wayward passions of the body.[18] The *soma*, sanctified and transformed, has a place in eternity, whereas the *sarx* has no place but is instead the battleground for spiritual warfare in the life of Christ. *Sarx* then, is the battleground of *askesis*.

Chrysostom believed both the *soma* and the *sarx* have an impact on how one is to live in Christ. The initiation into the kingdom of God, as adopted sons and daughters, begins with an image of Christ's death on the cross in baptism. One must die to the flesh, that one might be wholly transformed. The beginning of the life of ascetical battle starts with baptism and continues into the Christian life through the spiritual practices.

Now that the doctrines of God have been examined in light of *askesis*, the discussion can turn to the human being's role in *askesis*. The next section will shed light on the premodern understanding of anthropology through

---

16. Harakas, *Toward Transfigured Life*, 29.
17. For several examples of the use of *soma*, see 1 Cor 15:44; Luke 11:34; 1 Cor 12:12.
18. For examples of *sarx*, see John 3:6; Gal 5:17; Gal 6:8; Eph 2:3.

the patristic doctrines that concern human nature and *telos*, the role of the church, sanctification, salvation, and eschatology.

ST. JOHN'S THEOLOGICAL ANTHROPOLOGY AS IT CONCERNS ASKESIS

Now we are ready to move from the Eastern patristic doctrines of God that pertain to *askesis* to a discussion of theological anthropology. *Askesis* is the chief way in which the human being submits herself to God's healing grace. For this reason, the human aspect of participation with God, and the doctrines related to the human being regarding the transformation into Christlikeness, need to be discussed. Although the doctrines of sin and evil will be examined in chapter 5, *askesis* is meant to free the human being from spiritual bondage in order to allow the fruits of the Spirit to grow. At its core, *askesis* is a struggle against the effects of the fall. Since this is the case, theological anthropology is also a basis for *askesis*.

We begin with biblical revelation. In God's free and creative act of the will, he created humanity in his image and likeness. For the patristic teachers, the transformation by God's grace through *askesis* is understood within the context of humanity's image-bearing nature. Creation in the image and likeness of God implies that the *telos* of human ontology is to become like God. If this premodern concept is correct, then the only way for humankind to achieve true humanity is to achieve this end. What is good for God is good for humanity. The transformation into Christlikeness can happen only within the realm of the church, the very community where the Holy Spirit resides.

Moses was used as an example extensively by early church fathers, as they saw him as a prefiguration of Jesus Christ. Moses spent forty days with God on Mount Sinai to commune with him, and when he came down, his face was shining, radiating with the glory of God. He looked like God, he was more like him, and the people were afraid. He had to veil his face (Exod 34:28–35). Exodus is a prefiguring of Jesus Christ, and just as Christ is the first of us, Moses also prefigures humanity. The fulfillment of this is Matthew 17, on Mount Tabor. "After six days Jesus took Peter, James, and John (the brother of James) and led them up a high mountain where they could be alone. Jesus' appearance changed in front of them. His face became as bright as the sun and his clothes as white as light." Here is the revelation that Jesus, the Son of God, is God the Second Person of the Trinity, and a revelation of *theosis*: humanity is transformed by the presence of God. "We all with unveiled face, beholding as in a mirror the glory of the Lord, are being transformed into the same image, from glory to glory" (2 Cor 3:18 NKJV).

The Role of the Church in Spiritual Formation

Chrysostom's theological anthropology is not complete without a discussion of the church. The reason to discuss the church in terms of his moral education is that he did not see Christian spiritual formation or salvation as possible without life together in the church. The "little church" had to also be a part of the larger church.

So what did Chrysostom know of the church? Eastern Christianity holds that on Pentecost the church came into the world, "founded on a two-fold divine economy," that is, the work of the two Persons of the Trinity sent into the world—first Jesus Christ, then the Holy Spirit,[19] the first arriving with the incarnation, the second arriving at Pentecost. Hence, the church has a twofold nature, being both the body of Christ and the repository for the fullness of the Holy Spirit. Thus human beings can become truly human only within the church.

The church as the body of Christ is the first aspect of the church, her christological nature. Like Jesus Christ, the church is "theandric," both human and divine, and is the human nature "recapitulated by Christ and contained" within him.[20] It is also as the body of Christ that the church is a unity in any sense, the stable, sure foundation of the Rock. It is in this body that the Christian has access to the Holy Spirit.

This brings us to the second nature of the church, its pneumatological aspect. Each disciple, who is also a member of the body, contains the fullness of the Holy Spirit. The church is of one nature in Christ but a multiplicity of persons through the Holy Spirit. Maximus calls the church a *macro-anthropos*, as grace abounds from member to member in the growth of the church (think about this also in terms of the "little church"). Thus, in two aspects, the church is both a unity and a multiplicity, mirroring the Holy Trinity. "The Incarnation is the foundation of this unity of nature, Pentecost is the affirmation of the multiplicity of persons within the Church."[21]

---

19. Lossky, *Mystical Theology*, 156.
20. Lossky, *Mystical Theology*, 184.
21. Lossky, *Mystical Theology*, 176.

Spiritual Formation as Cooperation with the Holy Spirit through *Askesis*

Given the twofold nature of the church, the human being cannot undergo spiritual formation, as Chrysostom saw it, apart from the church. *Theosis* is the realization of the "divine prototype of humanness," and this realization does not happen in isolation but in community.[22] This highlights what is happening (or should be happening) within the Christian family. Chrysostom's theanthropic ethic, which is revealed in the church, is perfectionist in that it deals with the wholeness, or completion, of the human being in relationship, "looking to Jesus the pioneer and perfecter of our faith" (Heb 11:33–40; 12:1–2). Only in the consummation of the ages will the Christian and the church fully realize wholeness.

Nevertheless, the adopted sons and daughters of the Father within the church are called toward transformation in this present life, day by day. This new nature, this attainment of true humanness, of union with God, happens within the realm of the church. The church provides all the means necessary for the believer, who, in turn, works in cooperation with God in appropriating the grace acquired by the Holy Spirit through *askesis*.

That being said, did Chrysostom uphold merit-based salvation? By no means. As often as not, any discussion of working out one's salvation is immediately held in suspicion, if not denounced out of hand, because of the question of *merit*. However, within the theological tradition of the fathers, the question does not revolve around merit but around *synergy*, or cooperation. Indeed, Lossky states, "The notion of merit is foreign to the Eastern tradition."[23] This stream of Christian tradition does not view grace and human freedom apart from one another. Instead, the two are viewed as a simultaneous and reciprocal bond that manifest the same reality. For a better explanation, Gregory of Nyssa writes in "De Instituto Christiano," "As the grace of God cannot descend upon souls which flee from their salvation, so the power of human virtue is not of itself sufficient to raise to perfection souls which have no share in grace. . . . The righteousness of works and the grace of the Spirit, coming together to the same place, fill the soul in which they are united with the life of the blessed."[24] The work of the disciple, then, is not about meriting a reward but about lovingly and willingly submitting oneself to God's grace. This submission is the work of *askesis*, with the

---

22. Harakas, *Toward Transfigured Life*, 28.
23. Lossky, *Mystical Theology*, 197.
24. Gregory of Nyssa, as quoted in Harakas, *Toward Transfigured Life*, 104.

attitude of humility, ignorance, and repentance. It is kenotic, becoming empty of one's old self, that God might re-create a new self in his likeness.

The *telos* of the Christian life is the attainment of the Holy Spirit, and all works done in the name of Jesus Christ, in *askesis*, grant the Christian the fruits of the Spirit. All else, all good done for altruistic reasons, is nothing but splendid vice. So, Jesus could say, "Whoever does not gather with me scatters" (Rom 11:19, 23-24). Good deeds have no spiritual merit, and without the Holy Spirit's sanctifying presence that slowly transforms the doer of good deeds, the do-gooder is actually working against Jesus Christ. Other spirits are working through them, rival spirits that inevitably oppose Christ.

This is not a belief in grace as a reward for good deeds or meritorious acts of the free will. Instead, it is the doctrine of synergy, the idea of harmony between the will of God and the will of the human. This cooperation bears the fruit of grace, which is appropriated by human beings as they are "grafted" into the vine of Christ (Rom 11:19, 23-24). Cooperation, on the part of the human, means a constant turning to God, a continual life of *metanoia*, reorienting the self daily to be face to face with the glory of God, experiencing his grace.

This teaching is echoed by St. Macarius of Egypt when he says, "The will of man is an essential condition for without it God does nothing."[25] Furthermore, he describes grace as a yeast, growing within the Christian until it "becomes fixed in a man like a natural endowment, as though it were one substance with him."[26] The acquisition of grace is the aspect of *theosis* that entails human capability. Grace is acquired first through baptism, then through the spiritual struggles of *askesis* within the context of the church. A clarifying metaphor might be Noah's ark (1 Pet 3:20). The Christian (and the Christian family) is saved by obedience to God's plan, on the vessel of the ark (the church), through the waters (of baptism and *askesis*).

Salvation Concerns the Appropriation of Grace

Now I bring us to how Chrysostom understood salvation. Remember, the purpose of his moral/spiritual education was the salvation of the entire family. For Chrysostom, the beginning of the acquisition and appropriation of grace is *conversion*. In this way, his theanthropic ethic is soteriological. The Christian stands at the beginning of salvation, or wholeness, with conversion. The appropriation of grace, the constant attitude of turning—repentance—is the life of Christ, as the disciple grows toward union with God

---

25. Macarius, as quoted in Harakas, *Toward Transfigured Life*, 104.
26. Macarius, as quoted in Lossky, *Mystical Theology*, 199.

within the *macro-anthropos* that is the church. As the Christian bears good fruit, in cooperation with the Holy Spirit, she witnesses to the world, which is offered salvation. Every Christian, as she grows in the spirit, is called to high priesthood and so called to bring the lost around her to salvation. The glory of God emanates outward, and the world sees his splendor through the multiplicity of persons bearing the fullness of the Holy Spirit, the second aspect of the church.

The Final End of the Sanctifying Process

Chrysostom's idea of salvation leads to his eschatology. As the church increases, ever renewed and rejuvenated by the Holy Spirit as the yeast within the bread of the world (Matt 13:33; Luke 13:20–21), there comes a time, according to Scriptures, when the world will pass away (Matt 5:18; Mark 13:31; Luke 21:33; 2 Pet 3:10). This passing away will reveal the church as the eternal kingdom of God, manifesting the glory of God, as *all* will be changed, both physically and spiritually. Those who are united by grace in God through the sanctifying process will finally be fully united with him, while those who rejected God's grace and refused to have anything to do with him will remain apart from God, and his eternal light will be like a tormenting, inescapable fire.

I spent this entire chapter walking through Chrysostom's theology-ethic because it is so foundational to his understanding of spiritual practice in daily Christian life. Spiritual practice moves the practitioner through transformation as the Holy Spirit works within hearts and minds. This is what makes *askesis* so necessary an element to Chrysostom's moral education.

A final, clarifying summary of his theology might be better grasped through story. Martin Buber once said that he "made the fatal mistake of *giving instruction* in ethics."[27] He meant ethics cannot be explained or told but must be shown. Flannery O'Connor indicates this same truth when she writes, "A story is a way to say something that can't be said any other way . . . . You tell a story because a statement would be inadequate."[28] Chrysostom would agree stories give us the metaphors that unlock understanding. The following retelling of Jesus' parable of the wedding banquet emphasizes how premodern thinkers like Chrysostom understood the *telos* of the Christian life (Matt 22:1–14; Luke 14:15–24):

---

27. Buber, *Between Man and Man*, 105.
28. O'Connor, *Mystery and Manners*, 96.

> A certain man in the Gospels once pried into the marriage feast, and took an unbecoming garment, and came in, sat down, and ate. For the bridegroom permitted it. But when he saw them all clad in white, he ought to have assumed a garment of the same kind himself: whereas he partook of the like food but was unlike them in fashion and purpose. The bridegroom, however, though bountiful, was not undiscerning: and in going round to each of the guests and observing them (for his care was not for their eating, but for their seemly behavior), he saw a stranger not having on a wedding garment, and said to him, Friend how camest though in hither? In what a colour! With what a conscience! What though the door-keeper forbade thee not, because of the bountifulness of the entertainer? What though thou wert ignorant in what fashion though shouldest come into the banquet?—thou didst come in, and didst see the glittering fashions of the guests: shouldest though not have been taught even by what was before thine eyes? Shouldest thou not have retired in good season, that thou mightest enter in good season again? But now thou hast come in unseasonably, to be unseasonably cast out. So he commands the servants, Bind his feet, which daringly intruded: bind his hands, which knew not how to put a bright garment round him: and cast him into the outer darkness; for he is unworthy of the wedding torches. Thou seest what happened to that man: make thine own condition safe.[29]

Those who are baptized in Christ are invited to the great wedding, the metaphor for the kingdom of God. But if the one baptized in Christ fails to put on the holiness of God through the transformation into Christlikeness by way of *askesis*, like the guest at the banquet, she, too, will be thrown out. A life of repentance and holiness is not optional in order to enter the kingdom. This story embodies Chrysostom's teachings to parents, especially in his interpretation of Ephesians 6. This stresses that beatitude is the end of all human desiring and struggle. Chrysostom keeps this end in sight. "A pattern of life is what is needed, not empty speeches; character, not cleverness; deeds, not words. These things will secure the Kingdom and bestow God's blessings."[30]

Baptism is the beginning, the initiation by the Spirit into the way of life, but it is *only* the beginning. There is no immediate sanctification but a process of transformation, just like the little wooden puppet, who slowly changed through much difficulty and trial with the help of the Blue Fairy

---

29. Cyril, "Procatechesis," *Catechetical Lectures*, §3, in *Cyril of Jerusalem*.
30. Chrysostom, *On Marriage*, 69.

and mentors sent by her. For Chrysostom and many of his fellow church fathers, salvation is promised to those who persist, who endure a life of ascetic trials to the end. In this manner, salvation is truly worked out, by a disciple who fails and fails but always gets up with the help of the One Who Comes Alongside, the Spirit of Christ who grants grace and transforms the disciple.

THREE FORMS OF SPIRITUAL PRACTICE STRESSED BY ST. JOHN

Up to this point, I have presented the context of Chrysostom's theology. The ascetical struggle *is* the life of Christ. *Askesis* is the approaching of God through self-abandonment and the acquisition of grace by the Holy Spirit. Instead of a stable state of grace, Chrysostom's ethic sees grace as dynamic, as the Christian is always more or less in grace. The apophatic posture of humility, ignorance, and *metanoia* is the attitude of *askesis*. Life is a series of stumbles and falls for the Christian, in which he must get up again and again, redirecting himself to God through repentance, receiving the healing of forgiveness, and striving to cooperate with the ever-renewing grace of the Holy Spirit.

For Chrysostom, this pattern of life also includes the Christian family, for the same theological reasons that it is the pattern for the monk. *Askesis* begins the slow work of loosening the bonds that enslave, the passions, so that the Christian might experience true freedom to reveal God's grace and bear good fruit. The final goal of this process for the family is to become full members of the kingdom. Yet it all starts at baptism and the beginning of death to the old self through spiritual battle with the passions.

In the following sections, I will highlight the three key methods of spiritual practices prescribed by Chrysostom. First, however, a review is necessary on how many premodern theologians viewed the spiritual battleground where these practices took place. There will be a brief overview of the passions and *apatheia*, or the state of indifference sought through *askesis*. This review will be followed by a deeper look at the three main forms of spiritual exercise: prayer, fasting, and alms-giving.

Askesis as the Pursuit of Freedom from the Passions

At this juncture, it is necessary to explain the passions further and how Chrysostom perceived them, as it is the passions that *askesis* tames within the human heart. In chapter 2, passions were described as impulses, desires, or cravings that have overtaken and subjugated the human being. Yet there is more to it than this, and Evagrius Ponticus (AD 343 to 399) is a useful guide to a deeper understanding of this aspect of human psychology. Evagrius spent sixteen years in the desert of Egypt working out the passions, which he likened to a *pathos*—a disease or even a parasite on the human soul.

Evagrius was a controversial writer, even in his own time, and in later centuries, some of his work was censored because of its reliance on Origen. However, the spiritual insight he presents on human psychology rests on the wisdom he attained and nurtured from his other teachers. These include Basil the Great and Gregory of Nazianzus, and the two monks Macarius the Great and Macarius of Alexandria. Overall, he is a good representative of patristic teachings on spiritual exercises, passions, virtue, and vice. His teachings provide a useful framework for understanding the inner workings of the human soul. In his view of human psychology, the spirit/soul of the human being is composed of three powers: the *rational*, the *irascible*, and the *concupiscible*.[31] These powers are meant to work in harmony, and each contains its own "field of operation."[32]

Evagrius taught that, in order to function in accordance with their natures, each of these powers must work together to achieve their right ends. The rational power is the intellect, while the irascible and concupiscible make up the so-called irrational part of the soul. The concupiscible part is the desire for virtue; the irascible part, sometimes called the watchdog of the soul, fights to obtain virtue. The rational part, the intellect, allows for the contemplation of the good. Any disharmony within one of these parts causes the other two not to function properly. The rational power is supposed to govern the two irrational powers, which are prone to the passions. If the irrational parts of the soul become disordered, they take over and effectually blind the rational part's ability to function. The passions arise from the "misuse of what in itself is good."[33]

Evagrius divides passions into two categories. The first are the bodily passions—passions that are roused by the bodily needs of hunger, the sexual drive, clothing, or sleep. These are stirred up when the individual misuses what is natural to the body through giving in to temptation caused by some sensory object. A simple example is binge eating ice cream after being tempted by a Dairy Queen advertisement. A better example is drawn

---

31. Evagrius is borrowing from ancient Greek philosophy, as did his teachers. Plato and Aristotle both speak of the three parts of the soul, calling them reason, spirit, and appetite. In contemporary parlance, this would be belief, emotion, and desire.

32. Bunge, *Dragon's Wine*, 15.

33. Bunge, *Dragon's Wine*, 16.

from literature. Francesca, in Dante's *Inferno*, is a carnal sinner, one of the many who "subject their reason to their lust."[34] Dante, like Evagrius, sees the rational capacity as what gives the human being the freedom to control desire. Yet that exemplified by Francesca is notable for its passivity in the face of desire. She is driven by her irrational parts. Thus she is driven by them even in Hell: "The infernal whirlwind, which never rests, drives the spirits before its violence; turning and striking, it tortures them."[35] It is telling that, even grammatically, Francesca presents herself as a passive object instead of as a free agent capable of controlling her desires. Evagrius's prescription to cure a Francesca ailing from bodily passions is straightforward: fasting and abstinence. Use of the remedy teaches bodily self-control.

The second category of the passions is that of the soul. Evagrius considered these passions much more serious, as bodily self-control can be mastered at a relatively young age. On the other hand, the passions of the soul can haunt an individual even in old age. These passions are triggered mainly through our relationships with other people and include resentment, inordinate anger, envy, vanity, pride, hatred, and so on. Evagrius believed the root of these passions is the misuse of loving oneself. Only spiritual love, which is a multifaceted jewel of virtue that reflects meekness, kindness, compassion, mercy, etc., can remedy these passions. The *telos* of Christlikeness, which can be achieved only through the aid of the Holy Spirit, includes the "restoration of the natural operation *of all three powers of the soul* in accordance with their creation."[36]

God is the Great Physician, and transformation into Christlikeness is about mercy, healing, and restoration. It means freedom from sin and shame and offering one's new life to God in love and gratitude, just as Mary Magdalene did after Jesus healed her from total demonic oppression (Luke 8:2).

Achieving Indifference to the Passions through *Askesis*

Apatheia is a secondary goal of *askesis*. Chrysostom and his fellow teachers understood it as freedom from the passions. To become indifferent, or apathetic, to the passions that rule over a person was not a new idea, as the Stoics were the foremost philosophers to cultivate and promote this state of being. Yet for the Stoic, apathy is the primary *telos*, the goal of human happiness.

This is not the case for Christians. Indifference to the passions is a good thing for the Christian, but it is not the foremost goal: communion

---

34. Dante, *Inf.* 5:38–39, as quoted in Gragnolati and Webb, "*Dubbiosi Disiri*," 115.
35. Dante, *Inf.* 5:31–33, as quoted in Gragnolati and Webb, "*Dubbiosi Disiri*," 115.
36. Bunge, *Dragon's Wine*, 21.

and participation with God is the end and sum of human happiness. Yet *apatheia* is called for by Chrysostom, as it grants freedom from those snares in the world that hold back the disciple from achieving the real *telos*. In seeking *apatheia* through *askesis*, the fathers sought to imitate their Master. Jesus upheld three spiritual exercises for his followers to practice, and these three practices grant the Christian both freedom from spiritual bondage and, more importantly, freedom to draw nearer to God. They are the vehicles of cooperation with the Holy Spirit.

The First Spiritual Practice: Prayer

Prayer is the chief spiritual exercise for Chrysostom. Without prayer, there is no transformation into Christlikeness. Its most basic definition is communion and fellowship with God. The apophatic posture readies the disciple for *askesis*, the foremost exercise being prayer. When the Christian wanted to approach God in prayer, he was to do so with a mentality of humility, ignorance, and repentance. With this in mind, it is helpful to see what ancient practitioners of *askesis* said about prayer. *The Philokalia* provides an excellent source for their teachings.

Definitions of prayer are abundant in *The Philokalia*. Listing them serves to flesh out what communication with God entails. Evagrius teaches that "prayer is the communion of the intellect with God," which is the twofold practice of the virtues and contemplation. He further explains prayer as "the flower of gentleness and the freedom from anger," "the fruit of joy and thankfulness," "the remedy for gloom and despondency," "the ascent of the intellect to God," "the energy which accords with the dignity of the intellect; it is the intellect's true and highest activity."[37] Saint Mark the Ascetic explains "prayer is called a virtue, but in reality it is the mother of the virtues; for it gives birth to them through union with Christ." He also teaches that it "compromises the complete fulfilment of the commandments; for there is nothing higher than love for God."[38] If Mark is correct, then the actual process of praying is a manifestation of love, as the human being is in intimate relationship, perhaps even union, with God during this time.

Another voice, St. Theodoros the Great Ascetic, calls prayer "a spiritual weapon" and "converse with God, contemplation of the invisible, the angelic mode of life, a stimulus toward the divine the assurance of things longed for, 'making real the things for which we hope' (Heb 11:1)."[39] Maximus the

---

37. G. Palmer et al., *Philokalia*, 1:55–65.
38. G. Palmer et al., *Philokalia*, 1:128–33.
39. G. Palmer et al., *Philokalia*, 2:15, 25–26.

Confessor, on the other hand, defines it as a "petition for blessings bestowed by God on man with a view to his salvation and as a reward for the good inner state of those who make the prayer."[40] Makarios of Egypt says of prayer:

> The crown of every good endeavor and the highest of achievements is diligence in prayer. Through it, God guiding us and lending a helping hand, we come to acquire the other virtues. It is in prayer that the saints experience communion in the hidden energy of God's holiness and inner union with it, and their intellect itself is brought through unutterable love into the presence of the Lord.[41]

Makarios's explanation of prayer shows how closely *askesis* is rooted in the theology-ethic described in the first half of this chapter.

Another teacher, St. Gregory of Sinai, believed, "Noetic prayer is an activity initiated by the cleansing power of the Spirit and the mystical rites celebrated by the intellect," and also it is the "the preaching of the Apostles, and action of faith or, rather, faith itself." Not only does he see prayer as "faith itself," he goes further, saying, "Prayer is God, who accomplishes everything in everyone (1 Cor 12:6) for there is a single action of Father, Son, and Holy Spirit, activating all things through Christ Jesus."[42] This idea of "prayer is God" sees even the cooperation of the human being in *askesis* as fundamentally the work of God.

Whether the Christian can accept one or all these definitions, when it comes down to it, prayer is struggle. Communing with God is not as easy as it was for the first human parents in Eden before the fall. Instead of walking in the garden of paradise in the cool of the day, we are more like Jacob wrestling with the Angel of the Lord. Prayer is the foremost battle ground where the Christian fights the self, the demons, the world, and all their distractions. This makes prayer not only the foremost spiritual exercise but the most difficult to practice. Mindfulness and attention are needed, virtues to be cultivated for prayer.

The Second Spiritual Practice: Fasting

Fasting is the second spiritual practice mentioned by Chrysostom in "On Vainglory," and he encourages its practice not only to parents but to every member of the household, even the youngest. This might seem extreme.

---

40. G. Palmer et al., *Philokalia*, 2:207.
41. G. Palmer et al., *Philokalia*, 3:292.
42. G. Palmer et al., *Philokalia*, 4:237.

After all, children are still growing and need nourishment. But the fathers had a practical and healthy view of fasting, as will be shown by example below, and never encouraged extreme forms that would harm the physical health of the faster. Chrysostom also was preaching to an affluent congregation whose children were not in danger of starvation. If anything, these children might have suffered from an overabundance of food.

For Chrysostom and the other fathers, fasting was always to be accompanied by prayer, lest it be fruitless. Precedent for fasting with prayer is found throughout the Hebrew Bible. The book of Jonah reads that the people believed God and proclaimed a fast, and great and small alike put on sackcloth. The king of Nineveh commands public repentance in dust and ashes, saying, "'Let neither man nor beast, herd nor flock, taste any thing; let them not feed, nor drink water; but let them be covered with sackcloth, both man and beast, and let them cry mightily unto God.... Who knoweth whether God will not turn and repent, and turn away from His fierce anger, that we perish not?'" (Jonah 3:5–9 JPS Tanakh 1917).

King David responds to the crisis of his dying infant in fasting and prayer. "David therefore besought God for the child; and David fasted, and as often as he went in, he lay all night upon the earth." For seven days until the child dies, David will not eat. When he breaks his fast, he is induced to explain his behavior, saying, "And he said: 'While the child was yet alive, I fasted and wept; for I said: Who knoweth whether the LORD will not be gracious to me, that the child may live?" (2 Sam 12:16, 22 JPS Tanakh 1917).

Through the prophet Joel, God speaks to his people, urging them to repent and be saved, "Turn ye unto Me with all your heart, and with fasting, and with weeping, and with lamentation; and rend your heart, and not your garments, and turn unto the LORD your God; for He is gracious and compassionate, long-suffering, and abundant in mercy, and repenteth Him of the evil. Who knoweth whether He will not turn and repent." (Joel 2:12–14 JPS Tanakh 1917).

Notice the refrain in all the above examples of supplication and fasting? Using Esther as the culminating example, the queen commands the Jews of Susa to fast, just as she and her handmaidens fast before she steps foot into the presence of her husband and king. Fasting in this case is both a sacrifice and an offering to God. The book of Esther is striking for never mentioning God or prayer, at odds with the three previous examples. Yet the formula is the same in the narrative between her and Mordecai and in her actions, implying the author of Esther is purposely bringing these to mind, without explicitly saying she prayed.[43] There is a specific reason for omitting

---

43. That is the formula of fasting and supplication, coupled with the parallel

God and prayer, but the readers understand that this is happening and that God is present nonetheless. For as the story unfolds, the climactic suspense mounts and her days of fasting create an undertone of fear and tension, just as do the three days of Jonah within the fish, or the three days of Jesus in the tomb. No, God is never explicitly mentioned in this biblical text, yet the offering of prayer and fasting together make him manifest as the focal point of the narrative and the true Savior of the Jews in the face of genocide. God is hidden yet fully present in the fasting and praying of his people.[44]

In addition to being a sacrifice to God, fasting has certain physical benefits. It sharpens the mind, focusing its attention on the task at hand, making it a great aid in the effort to commune with God. Time spent fasting cultivates a much-needed ability, the habit of self-restraint. Evagrius says as much when he teaches on this subject: "We should examine the ways of the monks who have preceded us, and achieve our purpose by following their example. One of their many helpful counsels is that a frugal and balanced diet, accompanied by the presence of love, quickly brings a monk into the harbour of dispassion.[45] John Cassian viewed fasting as the key to cultivate the virtue of temperance and calls it "control of the stomach, the opposite to gluttony." However, the fathers did not give a single rule or standard for eating and fasting,

> because not everyone has the same strength; age, illness or delicacy of body create differences. But they have given us all a single goal: to avoid over-eating and the filling of our bellies. . . . A day's fast [is] more beneficial and a greater help toward purity than one extending over a period of three, four, or even seven days. . . . The Fathers handed down a single rule of self-control: "do not be deceived by the filling of the belly (Prov. 24:15. LXX), or be led astray by the pleasure of the palate."[46]

---

language of other scriptural texts with "who knows" always referring to God. "That Esther is not in the place of God, but is rather playing a role in a larger story in which God is himself the principle actor, is elegantly alluded to in the expression that Mordechai uses to conclude the sentence 'Who knows whether it was not for such a time as this that you came into royalty?'" (Hazony, *God and Politics*, 199).

44. Hadassah's slave name, Esther, is Persian for "star." Yet when this name is transliterated into Hebrew, it sounds like the Hebrew word *astir*, "I will conceal" or "I will hide." God uses this term in other texts: "I will never again hide [*lo astir od*] My face from them" (Ezek 39:26–29). Mordechai, in giving his cousin this new name as she is forced from his care, calls to mind both the concealment of Esther's heritage and the hiddenness of God (Hazony, *God and Politics*, 194–200).

45. G. Palmer et al., *Philokalia*, 1:53.

46. G. Palmer et al., *Philokalia*, 1:73–74.

Interestingly, the practice of fasting has a dangerous side, as it can cause vainglory to grow in the practitioner. Makarios of Egypt warned his fellow monks about this, saying, "Don't put your trust in fasting . . . it can produce 'in us the self-conceit of perfection.'"[47] Fasting, although a spiritual exercise, is fundamentally practical. "Fasting, while of value in itself, is not something to boast of in front of God, for it is simply a tool for training those who desire self-restraint."[48]

Spiritual mentors are needed when the spiritually young attempt to fast, as it requires a wisdom that might be lacking in the neophyte. Gregory of Sinai brings up this concern:

> Younger people cannot keep to a strict rule by weight and measure, so how will you keep to it? . . . If you eat too much, repent and try again. Always act like this—lapsing and recovering again, and always blaming yourself and no one else—and you will be at peace, wisely converting such lapses into victories, as Scripture says . . . . There are three degrees of eating: self-control, self-sufficiency and satiety. Self-control is to be hungry after having eaten. Sufficiency is to be neither hungry nor weighed down. Satiety is to be slightly weighed down. To eat again after reaching the point of satiety is to open the door of gluttony, through which unchastity comes in. Attentive to these distinctions, choose what is best for you according to your powers, not overstepping the limits. For according to St Paul only the perfect can be both hungry and full, and at the same time be strong in all things (cf. Phil. 4:12).[49]

The presupposition is that the young do fast, just as Chrysostom speaks of in "On Vainglory." The purpose of fasting, like prayer, is *apatheia*. Other early church fathers speak to this as well. Saint John Cassian says, "Food is to be taken in so far as it supports our life, but not to the extent of enslaving us to the impulses of desire. To eat moderately and reasonably is to keep the body in health, not to deprive it of holiness."[50] This added benefit shows the Christian care and concern for the *soma*. Again, it is underscored that the human body is also undergoing transformation in Christ, not just the spirit. The Christian is to strike a balance between both sides of their nature:

> When heavy with over-eating, the body makes the intellect spiritless and sluggish; likewise, when weakened by excessive

---

47. G. Palmer et al., *Philokalia*, 3:335.
48. G. Palmer et al., *Philokalia*, 3:267.
49. G. Palmer et al., *Philokalia*, 4:281.
50. John Cassian, as quoted in Harakas, *Health and Medicine*, 39.

abstinence, the body makes the contemplative faculty of the soul dejected and disinclined to concentrate. We should therefore regulate our food according to the condition of the body, so that it is appropriately disciplined when in good health and adequately nourished when weak.[51]

Still, the freedom from spiritual as well as bodily passions is important. Diadochos of Photiki teaches that fasting not only did not "deprive" the body of holiness, but that it was vital to the attainment of Christian virtue: "Self-control is common to all the virtues, and therefore whoever practices self-control must do so in all things.... What is the good of a man controlling gluttony and his other bodily desires if he makes no effort to avoid vanity and self-esteem, and does not endure with patience even the slightest affliction?"[52] Thus fasting is of limited use.

Just as fasting goes hand in hand with prayer, it is also a help to the practice of alms-giving: "By not eating too much or too richly we can to some extent keep in check the excitable parts of our body. In addition, we can give to the poor what remains over, for this is the mark of sincere love."[53] The money saved by not eating can be given to those who have no money to eat. This brings us to the third exercise.

The Third Spiritual Practice: Alms-Giving

Chrysostom is noted for his many homilies on alms-giving, wealth, and poverty. Although it is not his main focus in "On Vainglory," it is still a spiritual exercise he demanded of the family, because it nurtured generosity, mercy, and love. Another example of a Christian teacher who held this sentiment, Maximus the Confessor wrote this in his first century (a collection of one hundred short reflections) on love:

> He who loves God will certainly love his neighbor as well. Such a person cannot hoard money, but distributes it in a way befitting God, being generous to everyone in need. He who gives alms in imitation of God does not discriminate between the wicked and the virtuous, the just and the unjust, when providing for men's bodily needs. He gives equally to all according to their

---

51. G. Palmer et al., *Philokalia*, 3:281.
52. G. Palmer et al., *Philokalia*, 3:266.
53. G. Palmer et al., *Philokalia*, 3:266.

need, even though he prefers the virtuous man to the bad man because of the probity of his intention.[54]

Generosity and mercy are the foremost virtues attained through the self's denial of monetary wealth. Saving money was not seen necessarily as a good thing. Hoarding money out of fear for the future, for security, or the desire to become wealthy was considered another form of bondage. The Christian is to give, as any abundance is simply a gift from God, one to be spread and shared, even to those society considers undeserving.

Maximus also notes, "Almsgiving heals the soul's incensive power; fasting withers sensual desire; prayer purifies the intellect and prepares it for the contemplation of created beings. For the Lord has given us commandments which correspond to the powers of the soul."[55] Just as prayers and fasts are sacrifice, so too is the giving away of material abundance. Both fasting and alms-giving acknowledge that God is sufficient, that he is our wealth and our treasure. Food and wealth can be taken away through hard times. Alms-giving is a concrete reminder to put our trust in him.

Alms-giving can look different, depending on the giver. Ilias the Presbyter remarks on these differences: "A truly merciful person is not one that deliberately gives away superfluous things, but one that forgives those who deprive him of what he needs. Some men through acts of charity acquire spiritual wealth by means of material wealth; others renounce their material wealth altogether on becoming aware of the spiritual wealth that is inexhaustible."[56] Those who become wealthy grow spiritually through the giving away of their riches.

Most importantly, alms-giving is not simply about giving away money. It is the very manifestation of generous mercy. Saint Peter of Damascus explains this powerfully:

> The person to whom it is granted to keep the commandments gives not only his possessions but even his very life for his neighbor. This is perfect mercy; for just as Christ endured death on our behalf, giving to all an example and a model, so we should die for one another, and not only for our friends, but for our enemies as well, should the occasion call for it. Not that it is necessary, of course, to have property in order to show mercy. Possessions, rather, are a great weakness. Indeed, it is better to have nothing to give and still to be full of sympathy for all.[57]

---

54. G. Palmer et al., *Philokalia*, 2:55.
55. G. Palmer et al., *Philokalia*, 2:62.
56. G. Palmer et al., *Philokalia*, 3:37.
57. G. Palmer et al., *Philokalia*, 3:97.

Whether we have money to give away or not is moot. It is the spirit of generosity and compassion that is nurtured that is important to God. So even if we have nothing material to give away, a heart full of sympathy can manifest itself in our actions, such as visiting those in the hospital, prison, hospice, or fostering children in our homes.

SUMMARY

The collected wisdom of *The Philokalia* was used above to reveal Chrysostom's mentality concerning the methods of spiritual practice that he advises in "On Vainglory." These examples challenge present-day Christians, especially those living in affluent societies. Self-restraint is not a virtue in a bigger-is-better, keeping-up-with-the-Joneses, profit-driven, consumerist culture. Talking about prayer, fasting, and alms-giving is easy, but putting these into practice until they become habitual is not. How does the follower of Christ take the initial step toward spiritual transformation? The answer is a call for self-examination. One of Jesus' most famous statements from his Sermon on the Mount is "How can you say to another believer, 'Let me take the piece of sawdust out of your eye,' when you have a beam in your own eye?" (Matt 7:4 GW).

The second half of this chapter has focused on how to attend to the struggle with the world and its demonic hold over our lives, but any attempt to enter the battle has to begin with a careful inspection of the chinks in our armor and our weaknesses. Jesus calls for this self-awareness. Moving forward without spending time in introspection and prayer, asking God to show us our own sources of bondage, is like rushing into battle blindfold. Don Quixote was blinded by his romantic tales of chivalry, and we are blinded by our own passions, whatever form they take. But the Holy Spirit is the Great Enlightener. We must beg God for the ability to see ourselves clearly. A popular Lenten prayer does this:

> O Lord and Master of my life, take from me the spirit of sloth, despair, lust of power, and idle talk. But give me rather the spirit of chastity, humility, patience, and love to Thy servant. Yea, O Lord and King, grant me to see my own transgressions, and not to judge my brother, for blessed art Thou, unto ages of ages.[58]

Overall, the goal of this chapter was to flesh out Chrysostom's embedded theology-ethic, which is the theological context and foundation for his teaching on moral education in "On Vainglory." His understanding of *askesis*,

---

58. Ephrem, "Lenten Prayer."

God as Trinity, spiritual formation, and salvation illuminate his promotion of the spiritual practices as an element in the spiritual formation of the family. In this context, I fleshed out the theanthropic ethic through a deeper look at theology and a few metaphors buried in story. The second half of the chapter was my attempt to clarify the passions as they were understood by ancient Christian voices. The last section defined the kinds of tools (spiritual exercises) encouraged by Chrysostom and other Christian fathers.

The next chapter delves into Chrysostom's patristic understanding of the fall's effect on human nature and human capacities of morality in an effort to highlight the second element of his pedagogy, imitation, or *mimesis*, as a learning ability. The following discussion will explain the inner happenings of the human being as a free moral agent to clarify what is taking place when a person makes moral decisions. This discussion is foregrounded within the reality of a fallen world marked by sin, corruption, and death.

4

East of Eden

Imitation and Fatherhood

IN THE PREVIOUS CHAPTER, Chrysostom's premodern understanding of the doctrines of God was revealed as the basis for his understanding of *askesis* and moral-spiritual formation. In this chapter, I focus on his understanding of the doctrines that concern human capacities for morality after the effects of the fall. *Askesis* is meant to free the human being from the effects of original sin, that the Christian might then be free to transform into the likeness of the second Adam. The cooperation with the spirit through spiritual exercise transforms the human capacities, to restore them to what they were before the fall. It is with this in mind that we will examine Chrysostom's second pillar of moral education, emulation.

Recall that emulation includes the concept of imitation as well as modeling. For Chrysostom, the disciple (the child) was to imitate the behavior of the model. This is why Chrysostom tells parents to point out to their child which of his or her friends avoids going to the theater.[1] It is also why he stresses to parents to live virtuously: "The things that concern us are fair dealing, disdain of money and fame, contempt for what the many think honor, disregard of human values, embracing poverty, and overcoming our nature by the virtue of our lives."[2] Children are to imitate their parents'

---

1. Chrysostom, "Address on Vainglory," 117.
2. Chrysostom, "Address on Vainglory," 93.

ascetical struggle, which bears Christian fruit. As imitation is a human capacity, and the second element promoted by Chrysostom, we as parents need to understand how imitation is connected with the other moral capacities and how it functions, especially in terms of mentorship.

Just as chapter 3 situates Chrysostom's first building block within his embedded theology, I will situate imitation as a building block within the context of fallen human nature and a corrupted world. Although touched upon briefly in the last chapter, Evagrius's pathos—the disease of the human condition—will be described further in terms of morality and the unnatural state of creation post-fall. The first part of the following discussion describes human beings as morally free agents and the human capacities related to moral decision-making abilities. The second part focuses on the premodern theological doctrines of sin, death, and evil. The third and final section explains mimetic theory and how it relates to the human capacities, human freedom, and the passions. I then will address mimetic theory in terms of Chrysostom's education for the Christian family.

HUMAN CAPACITIES FOR MORALITY AS PART OF THE IMAGE-NESS OF GOD

This investigation of human moral capabilities begins with a return to the discussion of "image and likeness." I previously spoke of image-ness in terms of human ontology and *telos*. For Chrysostom the transformation into Christlikeness was the end for which God designed humanity. For now, humanity's "image-bearing" nature has to be examined to better understand *how* the human being was designed to reach this *telos*. This investigation starts by returning to the phrase's source.

The phrase "image and likeness" comes from the first chapters of Genesis, which explain the origins of human life created by God. For biblical ethicists, there is much debate over what the creation account means by "image and likeness." Some theologies consider these two terms as distinct concepts, while others conflate "image and likeness" into one concept. Whichever view one holds, it is tempting for theologians and philosophers to try to pinpoint exactly where the image-ness is located in the human being. However, attempts to determine which specific part of human nature is the image-bearing part are problematic. The theologian might take one or more characteristic or capacity of the human being, the *autexousion* (the will), for instance, and make this one aspect the key definition. This is a mistake, as "the image of God does not belong to any one part of the human make-up, but refers to the whole man in his entirety."[3] The position Chrysostom held was that the human being as a whole, male and female, is created in the image.[4] The question is not "what is the image of God" but "who." The Incarnate One is the true human being, as he fulfilled the human capacity to *be* human, the way Adam and Eve were intended.

> For the name Adam is not yet given to the man, as in the subsequent narratives. The man created has no particular name but is universal man. Therefore, by this general term for human nature, we are meant to understand that God by His providence and power, included all mankind in this first creation.... For the image is not in a part of the nature, nor is grace in one individual among those it regards; this power extends to the whole human race.... In this respect there is no difference between the man made in the first creation of the world, and he who shall be made at the end of all things; both bear the same divine image.[5]

This quote from Gregory of Nyssa reveals how he and others, including Chrysostom, understood the Genesis account. To Chrysostom, the entire human being *is* the image.

Given Chrysostom's understanding that the human being as a whole is in "the image" of the Creator, then in what way does being made in the image allow for moral agency? To answer this question, fallen humanity must be contrasted to *true* humanity. In trying to understand how a human being can become an ethical person, or a true human, a discussion of the moral capacities will follow, beginning with the necessity of moral freedom, before turning to the question of what innate capacities make such things as moral freedom and moral decision-making possible.

Chrysostom's Understanding of Moral Freedom and Personhood

A good place to begin a conversation on Chrysostom's view of human moral freedom is to recall John Steinbeck's retelling of Genesis in *East of Eden*. Although unappreciated by the critics of Steinbeck's time, this novel is now considered a classic because it touches upon the very themes of this

---

3. Lossky, *Mystical Theology*, 120.

4. Jesus Christ unites the different spheres of the cosmos to his own Person. This includes surmounting the natural division of human nature into two sexes, as seen in his birth by a virgin. The successions of unions are listed by Lossky, *Mystical Theology*, 137.

5. Gregory of Nyssa, as quoted in Lossky, *Mystical Theology*, 120.

chapter: sin, death, the fall, imitation, rivalry, and moral freedom. When Steinbeck uses his main characters to voice his understanding of this last concept, that of the human ability to discern and choose between right and wrong, he uses the Hebrew verb *timshel*. This term is in the subjunctive voice and means "you may." *Timshel* becomes the refrain of the entire book, from its first appearance at the halfway point of the story, to the last page of the book, because Steinbeck believes it to be true. *Timshel* does not exist in the Bible, and Steinbeck fudges the biblical account of Cain and Abel to some degree, but, nevertheless, he has his finger on a biblical concept that he teases out throughout the story. For Steinbeck, the human being may choose between good and evil.

The concept of moral freedom has been a stumbling block for Christians over the centuries. The question always arises, how much responsibility does the human being have over his actions? The theological tendency is to take a position in one of two categorical extremes when attempting to answer this question. One extreme is to place God's sovereignty over man as so central that the human being is completely passive and can only submit willingly (or unwillingly, in the case of the reprobate) to God's ultimate control. This tendency creates a dilemma, as it effectually makes God, instead of the human creature, the author of sin.

The opposite propensity is to demote God's role to such an extent that the human being is viewed as having practically total autonomy. Jesus, in this christological view, is typically reduced to nothing more than a great teacher or role model, not the resurrected Savior of the world who was and is victorious over sin and death and is the Second Person of the Holy Trinity. These descriptions are only the barest sketches of complex theological quandaries, which will be sidestepped by providing a third option, the option upheld by Eastern Christians in the tradition epitomized by John Cassian. It is this option that most concerns how to understand Chrysostom's embedded theological anthropology.

Contemporary thinker Christos Yannaras helps explain Cassian's position in his aptly titled work *The Freedom of Morality*. He begins with the definition of person. The human being is meant to be a person, Yannaras asserts, not an individual. Person comes from the Greek *prosopon*, meaning "face." Human beings are to "face" others in relationships. Christ's summary of the two greatest commandments reveals how the human is to relate face to face with others, namely in love (Matt 22:34–40). Therefore, *koinonia*, meaning both "communion" and "society," is highly significant in Yannaras's understanding of the person.

Yannaras relies upon the Greek fathers' understanding of *hypostasis* to further explain his use of the term *person*. This Greek word has two meanings: to exist or to subsist. In the sense of existence, *hypostasis* can mean to exist in general or to exist "by itself and in its own consistency . . . differing numerically from every other."[6] A person is not only one who faces another, but who is a *hypostasis*, one who uniquely exists for the purpose of *koinonia* with God and neighbor.

This premodern view of personhood contrasts with the concept of the individual who is a "segment or subdivision of human nature as a whole." A person is fundamentally *not* an individual in patristic thought. Why not? Yannaras explains:

> Thus the person represents a mode of being which presupposes natural individuality, but is at the same time distinct from it. Each person is a sum of the characteristics common to all human nature, to mankind as a whole, and at the same time he transcends it inasmuch as he is an existential distinctiveness, a fact of existence which cannot be defined objectively. Man's nature in general—mankind as a whole, as a biological species—can be defined objectively: it possesses will, reason, intellect, etc. But each human person exercises his will and converses and thinks in a way that is unique, distinct and unrepeatable.[7]

Thus, human beings are both *individuals*, in terms of a biological species, and *persons*, in terms of being "unique, distinct and unrepeatable." The fathers, including Chrysostom, saw the human being as a plurality in community in the sense of having a common nature as a whole and being unique and distinct, as persons.

If one understands that God has a personal existence, and that he is One Substance and Three Persons, then one can make the leap that the human being is also made in one substance (or essence) but with many distinct persons (*hypostases*). The person is created to be in community and to relate in love to others, just as God exists in a community of love. This understanding of persons makes morality an ontological question, one that is "identified with the existential truth of man."[8] This view of morality carries with it an innate soteriology. When the human person is saved, she becomes a whole person, truly human. At the center of all human need and desiring is this thirst for salvation, or wholeness. Morality then, has to do with the human capability of personhood. Without the freedom to become a person, one cannot be transformed into the likeness of God. The freedom of morality is essential to humankind's *telos*. For Chrysostom, the *telos* of humanity

6. Lossky, *Mystical Theology*, 51.
7. Yannaras, *Freedom of Morality*, 21.
8. Yannaras, *Freedom of Morality*, 15.

was also the *telos* of the Christian monk, the Christian married couple, and the Christian family. Moral freedom means having the ability to choose to cooperate with the Holy Spirit, yielding with love to the transformation into Christlikeness, and, finally, partaking of God in eternity.

Additionally, love and the freedom of love play an important role in this premodern theology. If God is understood as love, ontologically, then love is the supreme ontological category which "constitutes His being."[9] Human beings were created to be persons in order to meet the Creator face to face in love, being united both with Creator and with each other. Love, then, cannot just mean anything to anybody, a vague "good feeling," as Joseph Fletcher described.

Vladimir Lossky makes similar statements regarding this premodern teaching. Drawing from Maximus the Confessor, he understands the human creature as being different from the Creator in the sense that we are limited. The *telos* of a human being is outside of ourselves and something which we are tending toward "in a perpetual state of becoming." He continues: "Wherever there is diversity and multiplicity there is becoming. . . . God alone remains in absolute repose; and His perfect unmovability places Him outside space and time. If one attributes movement to Him, in His relationship to created beings, it is meant that He produces in creatures the love which makes them tend towards Himself, that He draws them to Him, 'desiring to be desired and loving to be loved.'"[10]

God has a personal existence and gives humanity, the epitome of his creation, personal existences as well, that each and every person might freely participate in God's personal life, drawn in desire toward him. Let us continue in the next section below to see how this view of personhood and individuality is understood in connection with innate moral capacities. I am building a foundation for *mimesis* and for how imitation works both spiritually and morally in the development of the child.

Human Beings Were Created to See the World Morally

Given Chrysostom's view that the human being was created with moral freedom, the next issue to discuss is how the moral capacities function. If the human being is morally free indeed, then what is at work to allow moral processing and decision-making to happen? When speaking of innate moral capacities, premodern thinkers like Chrysostom choose nature over nurture, in the sense that part of what it means to be created in God's

---

9. Yannaras, *Freedom of Morality*, 18.
10. Lossky, *Mystical Theology*, 98.

image is the very capacities that enable the human being to choose right from wrong, to distinguish between good and evil.

There are two inborn sources within the human that make the moral life possible. One, the *ethike orme*—ethical drive—is an inborn inclination toward the good. This ethical drive causes the human being to naturally view events, situations, and actions in ethical terms, without reflection. Put another way, it is a universal human tendency to see the world in terms of ethical categories, whether the individual means to or not. Some scholars believe this drive is automatic, noncognitive, and unreflective.[11] However, as the human being develops and matures intellectually, from childhood to adulthood, the ethical drive recedes to some degree, as the maturing human being is now reflectively and mindfully making ethical determinations.[12]

This leads to the second source, the *ethike aesthesis*—ethical sense. The ethical sense takes the determinations made with the ethical drive and makes evaluative judgments. It allows us to discern varying gradations of morality, not just the good from the bad, but the good from the better, the bad from the worse, and so on.

Human Beings Were Given a Self-Determining Drive

Understanding the ethical drive and the ethical sense helps illuminate the next drive, one that some early fathers refer to as the *autexousion*—self-determination. It is this drive that enables ethical freedom and separates the human being from the other animals. It is the means in which the human being can become an ethical person. "In the beginning He made the human race with the power of thought and of choosing the truth and doing right, so that all men are without excuse before God; for they have been born rational and contemplative."[13]

This fundamental aspect of the image-bearing nature has important implications for the historical church's teaching on anthropology, which will be addressed in the second section. The ability to attain ethical personhood will depend on something beyond what the autonomous individual can achieve on her own.

---

11. For further discussion of the ethical drive, see Harakas, *Toward Transfigured Life*, 98–101. Harakas relies on the work of Vasileios Antoniades as his key source on the psychology of the ethical drive and sense.
12. Harakas, *Toward Transfigured Life*, 98–101.
13. Martyr, "First Apology," in *Justin Martyr and Athenagoras*, 31.

The Conscience as a Human Moral Capacity to Be Cultivated

The next aspect of the image-bearing nature that must be carefully described is how Chrysostom understood the conscience. The term *conscience* is one of those ambiguous terms that has gained and lost meaning over time. If I went to the mall or a farmers' market and asked random people in the crowd what this word meant, I would get a wide variety of answers. Is it an outside force, something like Socrates's *Daimon* or Pinocchio's cricket, that somehow guides or enforces actions? Is it the acknowledgment of what ought to be done in terms of moral law, as the Scholastics claimed? Is it a faculty of the human mind, or some other innate ability, like intuition? Or is it the superego described by Freud, a construct created by society, or the conditioning of our nurturing as behaviorists would have it? When questions like these are asked, it becomes clear that this term, although widely used, holds different meanings depending on the user.

The biblical view of the conscience differs from these other competing definitions, and therefore an explanation of this difference is helpful. The conscience, as understood by Scripture, holds the perspective that it is a human moral capacity. More explicitly, it is a "moral expression" of the person as he naturally depends on both the ethical drive and ethical sense, the *autexousion*, intellect, emotion, social relationships, and life experiences. In the scriptural references concerning the conscience, it is described as the source of guilt and shame, as well as the sense of being separated from God, and therefore good, as in Genesis 3:7–10, the immediate aftermath of Adam and Eve's succumbing to temptation:

> Then the eyes of both were opened, and they knew that they were naked. And they sewed fig leaves together and made themselves loincloths. And they heard the sound of the Lord God walking in the garden in the cool of the day, and the man and his wife hid themselves from the presence of the Lord God among the trees of the garden. But the Lord God called to the man and said to him, "Where are you?" And he said, "I heard the sound of you in the garden, and I was afraid, because I was naked, and I hid myself."

In this biblical account, there is no doubt that the parents of humankind feel guilt, shame, and alienation from the Creator with whom they once walked in the cool morning hours. There is no conditioning or societal pressure to invoke these feelings of guilt, shame, and alienation. There are only the two and God, who made them. These feelings were a natural result of the ethical drive and sense already within Adam and Eve, and the conscience the expression of these senses.

The conscience as revealed in Scripture also acts as an inner judge. Adam and Eve accept their punishment as a consequence of their actions, just as David does when Nathan confronts him (2 Sam 12), or Judas Iscariot in the New Testament (Matt 27:3-4), leading to his suicide. Yet this inner judge also acquits the ethical person of wrongdoing in the face of accusation. Job is an example of an innocent person being condemned wrongly, as his own words to his friends testify, "Far be it from me to say that you are right; till I die I will not put away my integrity from me. I hold fast my righteousness and will not let it go; my heart does not reproach me for any of my days" (Job 27:5-6). Tamar, also, when first judged by Judah as immoral, is later vindicated, as he acknowledges, "She is more righteous than I" (Gen 38:26).

Jesus and the apostle Paul are the best examples within the New Testament on how the conscience works as a judge. When Jesus is struck by the guard, as Jesus stands in front of the high priest for questioning, he asks, "If what I said is wrong, bear witness about the wrong; but if what I said is right, why do you strike me?" (John 18:23). Paul speaks to this in Romans 2:12-16:

> For all who have sinned without the law will also perish without the law, and all who have sinned under the law will be judged by the law. For it is not the hearers of the law who are righteous before God, but the doers of the law who will be justified. For when Gentiles, who do not have the law, by nature do what the law requires, they are a law to themselves, even though they do not have the law. They show that the work of the law is written on their hearts, while their conscience also bears witness, and their conflicting thoughts accuse or even excuse them on that day when, according to my gospel, God judges the secrets of men by Christ Jesus.

Chrysostom echoes the New Testament witness of the conscience acting as a judge when he instructs, "Open the doors of your conscience, and behold the judge that sits in your heart."[14] Why does he encourage his congregation to open the doors to this judge? Because the judge is also a guide and a teacher. He writes, "In the conscience we have an adequate teacher, and one ought not to deny oneself the help which comes from it."[15]

The conscience is the hub of the entire moral life. Since it is the interaction of multiple capacities and life experiences working together, it is then

---

14. Chrysostom, as quoted in Harakas, *Toward Transfigured Life*, 109.

15. Chrysostom, *Homily on Genesis 54.1*, as quoted in Harakas, *Toward Transfigured Life*, 109.

subject either to refinement and enhancement, i.e., sensitivity to the Holy Spirit, or to the opposite: deformation, suppression, and desensitization. When working properly, the New Testament describes it as *agathe* or *kale* (good), *kathara* (pure), divine, and *aproskoptos* (clear). The New Testament has many terms for the dysfunctional conscience as well: *ponera* (evil), *asthenese* (weak), *kekavteriasmene* (seared), etc.

Without the conscience, the human being will have real difficulty being intimate with God on any level. As "it is the human ability to function ethically," then without developing the conscience, we cannot develop primary virtues such as the ability to judge the morally good from the morally evil.[16] The conscience needs to be educated and trained, just as fine motor skills are a human capacity that need practice to develop.

It is hopefully clear now why the conscience needs to be formed well in individuals, as a deformed, weak, or hardened conscience will seriously hinder the achievement of true personhood, that is, Christlikeness. Consequently, a person with an underdeveloped or seared conscience cannot become part of her social environment (relate to or "face" the other), even disastrously so, in the cases of those criminals who are described as lacking a conscience. A crippled conscience alienates the person from both God and fellow human beings.

The Premodern View of Natural Law

Now that the conscience has been defined, another aspect of moral thought, natural law, must be considered from a premodern standpoint. The idea of a natural law "written on our hearts" (2 Cor 3:3) coincides with the idea of inborn moral capacities, and as imitation will be examined as such a capacity and is a fundamental part of Chrysostom's moral framework, then something should be said on how he understood this concept.

In his "Homily on Anna," Chrysostom preaches, "We were given two teachers from the beginning, nature and the conscience, theirs being an impartial voice which teaches human beings in silence."[17] The section above on conscience explained how in one sense the conscience acts as a teacher or guide. Yet what does Chrysostom mean by nature as the other teacher that the human being has had since "the beginning"? Nature here simply means the inborn human capacities, which were discussed above as the ethical drive and ethical sense. It might be less confusing, and more fitting,

---

16. Harakas, *Toward Transfigured Life*, 35.
17. Chrysostom, as quoted in Harakas, *Toward Transfigured Life*, 118.

to call the natural law "the moral law." These human capacities are natural to humankind and were created for the reasons spoken of above.

In premodern Christian thought, the unwritten natural (moral) law goes hand in hand with the written royal law (or the ethical teachings of the Bible—both the Mosaic and the evangelical). Both laws—natural and written—were given to reveal different facets of the same reality.

THE FALL'S EFFECT ON HUMAN MORAL CAPACITIES

Now that we have discussed how Chrysostom understood human moral capacities and have considered them as part of what makes the human being an image-bearer, the question to ask is how the fall affected these capacities. To answer means uncovering how Chrysostom would have understood what evil is and how evil affects the human ability of self-determination. A short presentation of patristic thought on sin and death is in order. This will give context to Chrysostom's use of imitation as the second element to his moral and spiritual education.

Evil and Its Relationship to Self-Determination

Up to this point, I have centered the discussion on human moral capacities as understood by Chrysostom and his premodern contemporaries. Now I must frame his theological anthropology within the context of the fall. To do so, I turn our focus to the nature of evil. Evil in Scripture is often equated with the world or the flesh. Evil is also used interchangeably with sin. A simple definition that helps me understand what evil really is, is taken from Stanley Harakas, when Harakas says, "Evil is that which ought not to be, which ought not to exist, or if it does exist in fact, should not continue to do so."[18] In secular philosophy and other non-Christian worldviews, evil is sometimes seen as relative, necessary, or equated with passivity, femininity, or darkness. In dualism, it is viewed as equally powerful as good, a force that cannot be destroyed or ended. Yet all these differing philosophical and religious systems have one thing in common: evil is the nonfulfillment of the *telos*.

There are alternative views of evil, such as the Christian Science view that evil does not really exist at all and is just an aspect of good. The *meonic* view (literally, "not being") is a form of this concept. While the early fathers

---

18. Harakas, *Toward Transfigured Life*, 69.

would not agree with the Christian Scientist that evil is an aspect of good, they do teach that God is not the creator and author of evil. "There was a time when there was no evil," Athanasius writes, completely rejecting the philosophy that holds that evil has an essence or that it is a "necessary constituent of good."[19] Evagrius Ponticus echoes this philosophy in his battle against the Manichaean dualism of his time, writing, "There was a time when evil did not exist, and the time will come when it will exist no more. However, there was never a time when virtue did not exist and there will be no time when it will no longer be."[20] Maximus the Confessor holds in his *Ambigua* that evil is a "nonexistence" or, as Yannaras interprets, "a mode of existence contrary to existence, and contrary to nature since it fragments and destroys nature; it means separation from being and exclusion from life."[21]

So, what is the origin of evil if it ontologically does not exist? This is where the freedom of morality becomes a double-edged sword. Evil, morally speaking, finds its birth in the *autexousion*, that human capacity for self-determination that makes it possible to choose either the good or the bad. It is important to understand, when speaking of the *autexousion*, that it is not an imperfection. God deliberately created humankind with this capacity. Evil was never a necessary component to humanity. The self-determining capacity is not evil in itself but the means to moral freedom.

Sin as the Alteration of Nature

This premodern theological anthropology holds that the original sin of humanity's first parents was the misuse of their self-determination. Yannaras declares,

> The fall of man takes place when he freely renounces his possibility of participating in true life, in personal relationship and loving communion—the only possibility for man to *be* as a hypostasis of personal distinctiveness. The fall arises out of man's free decision to reject personal communion with God and restrict himself to the autonomy and self-sufficiency of his own nature.[22]

---

19. Harakas, *Toward Transfigured Life*, 71.
20. Evagrius, as quoted in Bunge, *Dragon's Wine*, 15.
21. Yannaras, *Freedom of Morality*, 35.
22. Yannaras, *Freedom of Morality*, 29–30.

This self-sufficiency, however, is an "existential lie," as the human being can never really fulfill her *telos*, which is personal relationship and communion with God, by choosing such autonomy. The result is a fragmented human individual, not whole, not safe, not *saved*. It is a fundamentally unnatural state of existence for the human being. This fragmentation of humanity's true nature—personal *hypostasis*—continues with every new birth, in every new generation.

Saint Augustine of Hippo explains moral evil in another way. Although he was discussing fallen angels, his words are apt for humanity's fall as well:

> If we ask the cause of the misery . . . it occurs to us, and not unreasonably, that they are miserable because they have forsaken him who supremely is, and have turned to themselves who have no such essence. . . . For when the will abandons what is above itself, and turns to what is lower, it becomes evil, not because that is evil to what it turns, but because the turning itself is wicked. Therefore, it is not an inferior thing which has made the will evil, but it is itself which has become so by wickedly and inordinately desiring an inferior thing.[23]

Sin (*hattat* in Hebrew, *hamartia* in Greek) means "to miss the mark." This suggests the misfire, the arrow that does not find the bull's eye. Other meanings and descriptions are equally as vivid, for example, straying off the path and becoming lost. Sin is a distortion or a bending, a turning, a rebellion.

As I noted above, Maximus the Confessor describes sin as a distortion, an alteration of nature that fragments creation. He describes two ways in which Adam and Eve's sin broke nature. The first was the blameworthy rebellion of choosing another will over that of God's will: "The intention of Adam's natural reason was corrupted first, and this corrupted his nature with it, by rejecting the grace of freedom from passions, and so sin came to be. The first and culpable act was the fall of the intention from good to evil."[24]

The second, which he characterizes as a blameless sin, is the distortion and fragmentation of all of nature and creation, not just humanity:

> But the second, the blameless alteration of nature from incorruption to corruption, happened because of the first. For there were two sins committed by the forefather when he transgressed the divine commandment: the one was culpable, but the other

---

23. Augustine, "What the Cause," §1.
24. Maximus, as quoted in Yannaras, *Freedom of Morality*, 34–35.

was blameless since it had been caused by the one which was blameworthy. The one took place when the intention voluntarily set aside what is good; and the other, when the nature involuntarily laid aside immortality because of the intention.[25]

In this conception of sin, what we think of as "natural disasters," "acts of God," and other neutral evils all are a result of death being born out of the alteration to nature caused by the original sin.

Thus, from the premodern perspective, *hamartia* is always associated with this alteration, not in terms of good and evil but in terms of life and death. The purpose of ethics for St. John is the restoration, renewal, and transformation of creation. Ethics is not simply another word for the theology of sanctification but is embedded deeply within *all* of theology, including soteriology and eschatology. Now we turn to the last innate human capacity and how it functions in moral development.

IMITATION AS A HUMAN CAPACITY AND HOW IT FUNCTIONS

There is another innate, automatic function of the human being that is not normally discussed by ethicists, but I believe it to be as important as any other human capacity. This is the ability to imitate, a function critical in understanding one of the three elements of Chrysostom's pedagogy for the Christian family, and so I will explain why it matters within the context of his theology. The concept of emulation, the imitation or surpassing of a model, is spoken of by him as a vital way for children to learn right from wrong. As emulation includes both the concepts of imitation and modelling, both ideas will be analyzed in the following pages. The first part will focus on the nature of imitation through the lens of mimetic theory, a contemporary theory that will give further insight into why Chrysostom viewed it as a foundational aspect of moral formation.

Mimetic theory will be discussed in terms of its relationship with the *autexousion*, the "irrational" parts of the soul, the passions, and original sin. The impact of negative mimetic desire on human morality will be discussed first, and then the chapter will end with a discussion and examples of positive *mimesis* and its importance to Chrysostom's moral education and the Christian family.

As mimetic theory is explained in the following few pages, I will show how this relatively new theory of human psychology and anthropology

---

25. Maximus, as quoted in Yannaras, *Freedom of Morality*, 35.

complements both the Christian moral philosophy and psychology of the patristic period as represented by Evagrius Ponticus and more practically by Chrysostom. The following explanation will hopefully give the reader a fuller, more comprehensive understanding of what was discussed in the previous chapter on Evagrius's three parts of the human soul and Chrysostom's teachings on the power of emulation.

The Development of Mimetic Theory

Mimetic theory was first introduced by philosophical anthropologist René Girard. Girard was one of the last intellectuals to offer a grand, teleological, and universal theory of humankind and be taken seriously. Indeed, in this regard, he was considered a throwback to the previous century. His views, particularly in ethnology, gained him many critics. Yet, despite this, his concepts have provided fuel for a wide variety of researchers in every discipline imaginable: from economics to ecology, evolutionary biology to theology, literary criticism to psychology, and so on. There are very few theorists who can influence both the humanities and the hard sciences, yet this is exactly what he did, and it is perhaps one of the reasons he has been called "the new Darwin of the human sciences."[26] The following section will explore his thought regarding psychology and anthropology to offer another facet to the question of the human as a free moral agent.

The wide range of Girard's thought is an important point to consider, as theologian James Alison points to the apologetic need for theistic theorists who are also able to analyze and interpret empirical scientific data in ways that enable the Christian to incorporate these conceptual frameworks into the larger Christian philosophical viewpoint of anthropology. Alison argues that Christians should have an independent account of anthropology that is both positive and critical toward the modern discipline. In what he terms "wisdom anthropology," Alison calls for a Christian anthropology that mediates between revelation and dialectical anthropology. The key mediating factor is mimetic theory, which he believes is "particularly suited to revelation, indeed is concentric with it, and . . . this can be shown by the way it illuminates the major doctrines of the Christian faith without any sort of reduction."[27] It is with this in mind that using Girard's ideas about *mimesis* as a human capacity extends Chrysostom's thought on imitation. More will

---

26. Michel Serres is attributed with giving Girard this designation. See https://violenceandreligion.com/rene-girard-2/.

27. Alison, *Joy of Being Wrong*, 25.

be said on this after a brief summary of Girard's three-part theory concerning human nature.

There are three conventions concerning human nature that Girard upturned. The first is the idea that human desires are autonomous. The second is that human violence is caused by differences. The third is that religion causes violence. These three concepts, he revealed, are interconnected, and although they seem self-evident, he considered them romantic lies.

The empirical psychology on which this concept rests can be observed in small children playing together. In a room full of toys, even duplicate toys, if one child is playing with a ball, the second child naturally will try to take the ball away. A tug-of-war ensues, and, frustrated, the children will begin to cry as they fight over the toy, even if the same exact toy is present and available. This is the fundamental aspect of human nature on which advertising and fashion hinge, the fact that what the human being desires is not unique but imitated. *Mimesis* is a human capacity, an aspect of the image of God that makes the human being different from the other animals, even higher-order, prelinguistic animals like dolphins and chimpanzees. This capacity concerns metaphysical, or mediated, desire. This is not the desire of fulfilling the basic needs of hunger, thirst, or shelter. This is the desire of acquisitive *mimesis*. This desire is not autonomous and is instead imitated on a model.

This leads to Girard's second claim, the concept of mimetic rivalry. Mimetic rivalry is what happens when an individual sees the model of his desire as the obstacle to the object of the desire. The model has become a stumbling block that both attracts and repels. The model of the desire returns the favor, and then there is an escalation in rivalry as violent reciprocation moves back and forth between the two rivals. These rivals become *doubles*. From the outsider's perspective, the two appear the same. There is no noticeable difference, for instance, between Romulus and Remus, or the two prostitutes who stand before King Solomon (1 Kgs 3:16–28), or two families in a feud, like the Hatfields and McCoys. The rivals believe there is a vast difference between themselves and the opposing rival, but in reality, they are merely imitating the other in an endless, escalating cycle, in a "fearful symmetry."[28] In simpler language, mimetic rivalry is just another phrase for vendetta or vengeance.

When one rival triumphs over the other, like Romulus's killing of Remus, a metaphysical appropriation is taking place, as one model assumes the identity of the other. It is the sameness of acquisitive *mimesis*, the mirroring of the other, that causes violence between people, not their differences. This

---

28. A phrase from William Blake's poem "The Tyger."

trait is what Girard considers to be ultimately human. Nonrational animals also strive against rivals for territory or mating privileges, but they do not harbor grudges or commit genocide. Animals have natural restraints that keep them from conducting something fundamentally human, *war*. Non-human animals cannot threaten the existence of the planet, the way human beings can through unchecked violence in warfare.[29]

So, how do human beings deal with the problem of violence? For this answer, one must look to the third claim. Girard challenges the common wisdom that religion causes violence with the next step in the mimetic cycle. J. Budziszewski, in his discussion of essence, explains that while rationality and animality are a part of man's essence, accidental qualities like civilization and literacy are not.[30] They are instead a by-product. Girard believed that civilization, beginning with religion, was invented to *restrain* violence. Violence to restrain violence, Satan to cast out Satan.

How does he reach such a conclusion? In his various writings, in which he draws from historical and anthropological sources, Girard often describes a scenario in archaic human societies. The scenario is as follows: returning to mimetic rivalry, the rivalry has surpassed two individuals and now expands to two tribes of people. The reciprocal violence has accelerated, escalating now to the point that the members of each group cannot remember how it began. The object of desire has virtually disappeared; all that matters now is retaliation. Things are so chaotic that hierarchies are flattening as class and status become meaningless and differences disappear.[31] One cannot tell male from female, beast from man. Society is now in a state of anarchy. The end has come.

Then someone in the crowd points to the cause of all the chaos, a single individual amid the fighting. This person is different: disabled, foreign, an orphan, etc. The crowd in an instant realizes that the person in question is the source of the contagion and mobilizes (hence, mob) to unanimously descend on this individual and lynch him. When this happens, peace returns, quieting a now unified people. The society, relieved at the end of violence, now understands that only a god could have cured the sickness that was plaguing them.[32] A new religion has begun, with rites to be repeated over and over again, whenever violent contagion threatens, in

29. Girard et al., *Things Hidden*, 85.
30. Budziszewski, *Commentary*, 9.
31. Whenever differences begin to disappear, the community is near collapse.
32. Girard called the victim the *pharmakos*, the classical Greek word meaning both poison and antidote (Girard, *Violence and the Sacred*, 94–98). In examining word meanings, Girard also discussed the Latin *sacer*, which means both holy and accursed, and the German *Gift*, which is both a present (in English) and a poison.

imitation of the original founding murder. The individual who was lynched is now worshipped.

Girard believed this scenario was behind every origin myth (always told from the perspective of the murdering collective and therefore both hidden-in-plain-sight and legitimized) and behind every founding of an ancient civilization. The ritual sacrifices of the new religion always imitate the original cure to restrain the epidemic of violence from spreading. This "scapegoat mechanism" became the primary accidental quality of humankind's essential nature and is the threshold of humanization. It is also that which speaks to the question of signs and language, which allow the human being to reflect on choices and the past in a way other animals cannot. Think of this in terms of what we have discussed concerning the freedom of morality and making moral choices. If mimetic theory is correct, then imitation is fundamental in the ability to self-reflect and make ethical decisions.

Now the last convention has been overturned: violence causes religion. Religion is actually the cure and the binding restraint. Girard would flesh out his theory in later works, arguing that the reason human beings do not have new gods and myths is because this cycle only worked when humanity was not aware of it. Once someone came who revealed that the single victim was in fact *not guilty* of what the mob accused him before the act of collective murder, the remedy no longer worked. This is one reason Girard's theories are so controversial, as he held up the Bible and especially Christian revelation as the leavening over time that made humanity so sensitive to the innocence of the victim.[33]

So now I have discussed why imitation is such a fundamental part of what makes the human being a rational animal distinct from other animals. The unsung discovery of mirror neurons—"mimesis built into the human brain"—has caused many researchers in the area of neuroscience and developmental psychology to either implicitly or explicitly confirm Girard's claims.[34]

Return for a moment to Steinbeck's *East of Eden*. The novel portrays several examples of mimetic theory, particularly the scapegoat mechanism and mimetic rivalry. With the character Cyrus as his mouthpiece, Steinbeck explains the phenomenon of scapegoating and collective violence, using the

---

33. He argues that the Bible is the only source of ancient documents that reveal the innocence of the single victim, culminating in the passion account. He calls these persecution texts, which includes many of the psalms, Job, the deaths of John the Baptist and the apostle Stephen, etc. This effects his view of atonement, which is similar to *Christus Victor*.

34. Haven, *Evolution of Desire*, 219.

army as a stand-in for civilization, ritual, and the crowd. Cyrus says this to his son, Adam, whom he is forcing into the army:

> "I'll have you know that a soldier is the most holy of all humans because he is the most tested—the most tested of all. I'll try to tell you. Look now—in all of history men have been taught that killing of men is an evil thing not to be countenanced. Any man who kills must be destroyed because this is a great sin, maybe the worst sin we know. And then we take a soldier and put murder in his hands and we say to him, 'Use it well, use it wisely.' We put no checks on him. Go out and kill as many of a certain kind of classification of your brothers you can. And we will reward you for it because it is a violation of your early training . . . They'll first strip off your clothes, but they'll have to go deeper than that. They'll shuck off any little dignity you have—you'll lose what you think of as your decent right to live and to be let alone to live . . . You can't even wear a scrap or pin a note on your breast to say, 'This is me—separate from the rest . . . .' After a while," said Cyrus, "you'll think no thought the others do not think. You'll know no word the others can't say. And you'll do things because the others do them. You'll feel the danger in any difference whatever—a danger to the whole crowd of like-thinking, like-acting men."
>
> "What if I don't?" Adam demanded.
>
> "Yes," said Cyrus, "sometimes that happens. Once in a while there is a man who won't do what is demanded of him, and do you know what happens? The whole machine devotes itself coldly to the destruction of his difference."[35]

For Cyrus, the military is civilization, with all its rules and rituals, and the one who is different is quickly crushed by the unanimity of the crowd. Soldiers are sacred, and the hardships endured, both physically and spiritually, are purifying. Cyrus himself is the voice of the crowd and, because he loves him, is ready to sacrifice his son Adam on the altar of the army.

The father's love for Adam causes the younger son, Charles, to burn with envy and murderous hatred. The whole character of Charles is defined by mimetic rivalry. Charles beats his older brother nearly to death. When asked why, Adam tells his father the truth, "He doesn't think you love him."[36] Charles cannot stop seeing his brother as the obstacle to the object of his desire, his father's favor. The drama is repeated and intensified with Adam's own twin sons, Cal and Aron, eventually leading to Aron's death. Steinbeck's

---

35. Steinbeck, *East of Eden*, 24–25.
36. Steinbeck, *East of Eden*, 32.

entire drama unfolds with the story of Cain and Abel, repeating cyclically through the generations.

The above anthropology reveals another aspect of the fall that distorted the natural mimetic capacity of the human being, a part of the image-bearing nature of God, with which imbued his creature. Portrayed vividly in Steinbeck's retelling of Genesis, the ugliness of mimetic rivalry and envious mimetic desiring is something with which the Christian family will struggle, as does every human being after the fall. Part of the reason for *askesis* is not just to free the Christian from the impulses, cravings, and addictions that enslave but from the negative desiring that causes us to rage against our brothers and sisters. It is only with God's transformative grace through *askesis* that positive *mimesis* becomes possible.

How Mimesis Corresponds with the Passionate Parts and Self-Determination

Where does mimetic desire get placed within the overall portrait of the human moral capacities as understood by premodern theologians? The answer may lie within such theologians' view of basic human psychology. *Mimesis* is a part of what Evagrius calls the irrational part of the human soul, which is made up of both the concupiscible and irascible parts of the soul. Concupiscence is defined as a type of desire that allows the human soul, when in good working order according to its nature, to desire virtue. Mimetic desire is described by Girard as a neutral innate capacity, one that can be positive if directed toward a good object/external mediator, or negative, as in the case of acquisitive mimetic desire, which is focused on a bad object/internal mediator.[37] Concupiscence, which is the desiring part of the soul, is nothing other than mimetic desire.

The irascible (emotional) power of the soul is the power from which anger—both righteous and wayward—is born. This power is naturally combative, and it is meant to protect the soul. Evagrius describes irascibility as the power that, when used correctly, battles demons. When used wrongly, it is the wrath that is waged against the neighbor. This correlates with Girard's description of mimetic rivalry, which views the other as an obstacle or enemy. Mimetic rivalry is the expression of the concupiscent and irascible parts run amok, fueling one another. The intellect is blinded, and the whole

---

37. An external mediator is distant from the imitator. For example, a fictional character in a book or an ancient saint are both distant from the one who is using them as a model. An internal mediator is someone who is close to the one imitating, like a sibling, coworker, or neighbor.

situation can be described as a runaway team of horses with a blinded and panicked driver at the reins.

When the irrational part of the soul, which contains these two powers, is out of control, the rational part (the intellect) is darkened. Desire, incited by some object, gives fuel to anger, and "provoked irascibility blinds the beholder."[38] This matches Girard's concept of the mimetic crises. He claims that the violent outburst of scapegoating in the advanced stages of mimetic rivalry could happen only if the crowd were unaware of what it was doing.[39] He recalls Jesus' prayer on the cross, "Father, forgive them, for they know not what they do" (Luke 23:24).

The key element Girard adds to what is already described in detail by Evagrius is imitation. Chrysostom, in discussing imitation as a teaching mechanism for children, says it "is a more potent instrument than fear or promises or aught else."[40] Gabriel Bunge, in analyzing Evagrius's work on the passions (anger, in particular), writes that the passions, when "linked to the person of a fellow human being, can all too often be sparked by material objects these people possess or which are connected to them. They incite in some way our concupiscence, and this fuels anger."[41] His "in some way" is exactly the human being's inborn capacity to imitate. This capacity is not ruled by the intellect. Remember Metzloff's quote from chapter 1: *"Humans imitate before they can use language; they learn through imitation but don't need to learn to imitate."*[42] Chrysostom would tell us, concerning imitation, it is only through *askesis* that the rational part (the intellect) learns to control the irrational part of the human soul. Imitation is not learned, but it can be intentionally directed toward positive models of desire.

Imitation of the Wrong Model as the Cause of Original Sin

> Now the serpent was more crafty than any other beast of the field that the Lord God had made. He said to the woman, "Did God actually say, 'You shall not eat of any tree in the garden'?" And the woman said to the serpent, "We may eat of the fruit of the trees in the garden, but God said, 'You shall not eat of the fruit of the tree that is in the midst of the garden, neither shall

---

38. Evagrius Ponticus, *Kephalaia Gnostika*, as quoted in Bunge, *Dragon's Wine*, 19.

39. The crowd perceives itself to be righteously attacking a threat, the cause of the crisis.

40. Chrysostom, "Address on Vainglory," 117.

41. Bunge, *Dragon's Wine*, 19.

42. Meltzoff, "Out of the Mouths," 59.

you touch it, lest you die.'" But the serpent said to the woman, "You will not surely die. For God knows that when you eat of it your eyes will be opened, and you will be like God, knowing good and evil." So when the woman saw that the tree was good for food, and that it was a delight to the eyes, and that the tree was to be desired to make one wise, she took of its fruit and ate, and she also gave some to her husband who was with her, and he ate. Then the eyes of both were opened, and they knew that they were naked. (Gen 3:1–7)

To Girard, the original sin of the above narrative was caused by misplaced desire. His interpretation of the Decalogue in the first chapter of *I See Satan Fall like Lightning* confirms this, as he points to the second table of the commandments, the sixth to ninth commandments (Exod 20:13–16), as simply forbidding the most serious acts of violence against one's neighbor. The last commandment, however, does not forbid an act but desire itself (Exod 20:13–17). The tenth commandment is a summary of all the others defined by their acts. Simply put, people are not to murder, steal, lie, cheat, or desire anything that does not belong to them, because it is the motivating cause of the violence done to others. The word *covet* to Girard is a misleading translation of desire. This desire is not some rare form of desire we only sometimes feel but the most basic to our nature—imitative desire that leads to rivalry and, ultimately, violence.

For Girard, the scene in the garden was the first moment human beings succumbed to mimetic desire and then to mimetic rivalry. The serpent offers himself as a model for Adam and Eve's desire. The temptation "to be like God" meant becoming like God without God's will, essentially to become God's rival, just like the serpent. It is literally as James puts it in James 1:13–15, "Let no one say when he is tempted, 'I am being tempted by God'; for God cannot be tempted with evil, and he himself tempts no one. But each person is tempted when he is lured and enticed by his own desire. Then desire when it has conceived gives birth to sin, and sin when it is fully grown brings forth death."

Returning to the human capacity for self-determination, recall many of the early fathers' viewpoint on original sin: the overall entrance of death and decay into the created order was misdirected self-determination. Girard is correct in that temptation is a matter of modeling one's desire after another's. This is what Jesus' temptation in the wilderness looked like, Satan giving him desires to imitate—bread, worship, and dominion over the world—all without the terrible death of crucifixion and all opposed to the will of God, Satan's rival (Matt 4:1–11; Mark 1:12–13; Luke 4:1–13). The first parents gave into this temptation and set the course for future generations.

All the inborn capacities became distorted and broken, making it ever easier after this point to desire the wrong *telos* and remain fragmented "individuals" of humanity, instead of whole, ethical persons. Through Jesus' obedience to the will of the Father, the path to God's *telos* for humanity opened as it had not been open since prior to the fall. As we begin to discuss imitation in the positive sense used by Chrysostom, keep in mind this discussion of how much power this capacity has to distort our relationships through envy and violent anger. Sibling rivalry, ever present in the family with multiple children, can be minimized through Chrysostom's prescription of parents and spiritual mentors modeling Christian virtue.

POSITIVE MIMESIS AND ST. JOHN'S USE OF BIBLICAL MODELS

Although Girard theorizes that human aggression is caused by the innate human capacity to imitate, he still believed that *mimesis* was neutral. This neutrality is like what is seen with the self-determination, a double-edged sword that when misused becomes sinful. Positive *mimesis*, however, is the right use of this capacity. It is the way babies learn to talk and walk, and it is the way young children learn, as they observe their parents.

In an interview, Rebecca Adams asked Girard whether mimetic theory could account for "desire on behalf of the Other—for nonviolent, saintly desire—as an excess of desire rather than a renunciation of desire."[43] He answered, "Wherever you have that desire, I would say, that really active desire for the other, there is some kind of divine grace present."[44] He elaborates on this idea in one of his later books:

> Christianity invites us to imitate a God who is perfectly good. It teaches us that if we do not do so, we will expose ourselves to the worst. There is no solution to mimetism aside from a good model ... we have no choice but to imitate Christ, imitate him to the letter, do everything he says to do. The Passion reveals both mimetism and the only way to remedy it. Seeking to imitate Dionysus, to become a "Dionysiac philosopher," as Nietzsche tried to become, is to adopt a Christian attitude in order to do the exact opposite of what Christianity invites us to do.[45]

---

43. Girard, *Girard Reader*, 63.

44. Girard, *Girard Reader*, 65.

45. Girard, *Battling to the End*, 101. Girard also said in a later interview, "I am just repeating here what Nietzsche said, although I am doing it *in reverse*. Nietzsche took sides with the persecutors. He thinks he is against the crowd, but he doesn't realize that

We cannot resist imitating, but we *can* convert away from imitating Dionysus (the world). For Girard, the simple renunciation of desire is not the answer, as it is in Buddhism, but is instead always imitation of a positive model. Identification with Jesus Christ, imitating him as our model, puts us in the proper relationship and distance between other human beings and the greatest Being. Paul's exhortation to "imitate me, then, just as I imitate Christ" (1 Cor 11:1 GNT) is the key, as are "the positive things, the fruits of the spirit: love, joy, peace, and so forth."[46]

In a keynote lecture, "The Embodied Logos," Rowan Williams asserts that freedom from the twin passions of anger (aggression) and materialism (acquisitive *mimesis*) was of great importance for the Christian witness in the world. This takes us in a full circle, from imitation back to Chrysostom, *askesis*, and the emulation of models. Spiritual training and mentorship opens up the believer to the work of God's grace through the power of the Holy Spirit. As discussed in the prior chapter, baptism is the first step, the initiation into life in the kingdom. Dying to the self, the individual, is possible only in the church, the vehicle of the Holy Spirit. The church gives athletes of Christ all the mentors and training that are needed. It is through spiritual exercise and mentorship that we can tend to our soul, allowing the fruit of the Spirit to grow.

The Emulation of Christlike Models

Given the powerful innate capability of imitation, Chrysostom encourages parents to become models of faith and Christian virtue. He also stresses telling Bible stories and giving children biblical models to follow. The Bible gives a plethora of models to whom to look, ordinary men and women whose lives were transformed forever by their relationship with the Triune God. Moses was already mentioned, and for good reason. Both Paul and later church fathers held him up as the model of transfiguration. Although he had many faults, Moses drew near to God, prefiguring both Jesus Christ and all human beings who seek God's face. Many patristic thinkers struggled with the Hebrew Scripture over the ways Christians could emulate models who often had deep character flaws but were considered righteous in the eyes of God, like King David. Despite this struggle, Chrysostom and some of his peers continued to offer up these biblical figures as models to emulate.

---

the Dionysian unanimity *is* the voice of the crowd . . . . He does not see that the dionysiac is the spirit of the crowd, of the mob, and the Christian is the heroic exception" (Girard et al., *Evolution and Conversion*, 142).

46. Girard, *Girard Reader*, 63.

Models were also drawn from the Christian New Testament, including Mary, the mother of Jesus. The church is called to imitate Mary, because through her love, obedience, humility, and faith in God, Mary responds to God's call by being the first to become the temple of the Holy Spirit (Luke 1:35). In a way, she is the embodiment of positive *mimesis*, "giving her life to the Other and fulfilling her life in him."[47] This is the complete denial of the self, yet at the same time transcendence into the *real* self, the true person God created her to be.

In doing so, the second Eve fulfilled what Schmemann called "the *womanhood* of creation" and what Paul called the great mystery of Christ and his church.[48] The acceptance of the woman of the Bridegroom is not blind or passive but loving and active. This is what Mary models for the church, and indeed every member of the church in turn is to imitate this active love, this acceptance of the Holy Spirit into hearts and lives, to be his very temple (1 Cor 6:19).

Saint Mary Magdalene is another life-giving model for the disciple of Christ. The New Testament is very specific concerning Mary's prior life before Jesus healed her. We are told that she was possessed by seven demonic spirits (Mark 16:9). The number seven signifies completion, as it does in Genesis with the creation of the universe. Mary of Magdala was *entirely* oppressed, *completely* given over to satanic powers (Luke 8:2). When Jesus healed her, those who had known her before must have marveled at the transformation. From this moment on, she devotes her whole life and being to following her Savior. She follows him on the road to the cross, alongside his mother, even as eleven of his closest disciples abandon him. She is one of the myrrh-bearers, the first to enter his tomb (Mark 16:1–8). Finally, she is the first person to see and speak with the risen Christ (Mark 16:9–11; John 20:10–18). Tradition tells us that she witnessed concerning his resurrection for the rest of her life, and she is considered equal to the apostles by the church fathers.

Just as every Christian is a Saul of Tarsus, a former persecutor of Christ, every Christian is also called to follow Mary Magdalene's example as fully living a life transformed by the healing power and mercy of the Spirit of Christ, no longer subjected to the power of demonic forces. The rabbis teach that God favored Abel over Cain, because, as a farmer, Cain worked so hard in the fields that his entire focus remained on earthly matters. Abel, on the other hand, was a shepherd, which meant he spent long hours of the night in silence, contemplating his Father. Like Abel, another Mary—St. Mary of

---

47. Schmemann, *For the Life*, 102.
48. Schmemann, *For the Life*, 102.

Bethany—sat quietly at the feet of her Lord, listening and contemplating, devoted to her relationship with him (Luke 10:38–41). This devotion and attention, this seeking first the kingdom, is what both Marys model.

The martyrs are also positive models. Saint Stephen, the first of the disciples to die like Christ, gives us the example that might in time be followed (Acts 7:54–60). Saint Perpetua and St. Felicitas, too, are early Christian martyrs who died in the Roman arena after imprisonment. Both were mothers, one even giving birth in prison. Their torturous circumstances and their faith witness to everyone who saw them, revealing the cost of following Jesus. "Now I suffer what I suffer; but then Another will be in me who will suffer for me, because I too am to suffer for him."[49]

Fatherhood as a Metaphor for Mentorship

Chrysostom, in speaking of emulation, also has mentorship in mind. The parents are to show their young how to live through their own actions and deeds. Theologian Vigen Guroian has devoted his time to studying this aspect of Chrysostom's work. In his discussion of mentorship, he bemoans the fact that the egalitarianism pushed in Western society biases us against pure mentorship. He points to the children's book *Bambi: A Life in the Woods* as the truest depiction of mentorship one can find. Unfortunately, this classic is hidden by both the bias against authority that has grown in our culture and Disney's obscuration of the true contents of the story.

In his work on children's literature, Guroian explains that true mentorship is needed for the disciple, and the very nature of mentoring automatically implies an inequality between the mentor and the mentee. First, it is the mentor who must willingly choose to train the pupil, but again, current society would have it the other way around. Regardless of society, the church is where the young Christian is supposed to find a mentor who gives her life as an example of how to live in the faith. As noted in the introduction, for the family, the parents are to willingly mentor their children in what it means to be a follower of Christ. This mentorship is shown through the metaphor of the old stag and the young, between the father and the son in *Bambi*. The mentor is to teach his young disciple how to spot the dangers of the world and how to be alone and should cultivate the right virtues for the pupil to habituate. For the Christian family, this is the call to fathers and mothers to mentor their young children in the life of Christ. For the church,

---

49. The record of Felicita's response to her prison guards who taunt her during her labor (Malone, *First Thousand Years*, 111).

it is for the spiritual fathers and mothers to come forward and mentor the newly baptized "children."

Finally, the purpose of mentorship is to pass on a certain way of doing things, a certain way of life:

> In contrast to the spirit of modern educational theory, in the mentor/mentee relationship there is no distinction between method and content. By means of physical gesture, tone of voice, and behavior, the mentor communicates his special knowledge and skill and also a piece of his own character. There is no such thing in this relationship as being informative without also being formative.[50]

Is this not the very description of how Jesus taught his disciples? As Guroian notes, this is not a modern way of thinking about education and the young. This is classical, in line with Aristotle's view of moral formation, which is why this explanation fits so well within Chrysostom's vision of how the parent is to mentor. This is the biblical pattern, that a life lived a certain way *is* the teaching. This is why the crowd exclaims concerning Jesus' miracles, "What sort of new teaching is this?" (Mark 1:27 NLT).

East of Eden portrays fathers and sons repeating the same mistakes as the first human family: sons vying for the love of their father, fathers grieving over lost loves, and, ultimately, fathers like the one in the parable of the prodigal son, who will run to the lost children who have come home (Luke 15:11–31). Chrysostom and René Girard both uphold imitation as a foundational way in which the human being learns. This key capacity can be cultivated, along with the conscience, in the child through mentorship by father and mother or by those who choose to take on these roles. Another premodern thinker, Dante Alighieri, presents two parental figures, Virgil and Beatrice, as his guides to salvation throughout *The Divine Comedy*.[51] This was the ancient path of wisdom, the way of passing down the most important lessons in life to the next generation, Chrysostom's metaphor of the golden cord.

---

50. Guroian, *Tending the Heart*, 104.

51. "His theological and poetic construction reveal the fundamental and inescapable role played by human models, both real and literary. In fact Dante describes purgatorial souls mediating upon positive and negative examples taken from the Bible and classical mythology. We are born within a human world and we are nurtured and directed by human models" (Antonello and Webb, *Mimesis, Desire*, xxxii).

SUMMARY

In this chapter, I emphasized how image-bearing involves the human being in her entirety and is not one single attribute or capacity. The idea of Christlikeness as the transformation from the human individual into the ethical person, the true human, is part of God's *telos* for humanity, that humanity might participate with him throughout eternity. Moral freedom is a part of this image-bearing nature of humanity. Freedom does not mutually exclude God's grace or enable the human being to "merit" grace or salvation through moral acts. Instead, moral freedom harmonizes with grace and bears witness to the same spiritual reality and mystery. Moral freedom is a necessity, for without it, the human individual could not seek union with God, through cooperation with the Holy Spirit. Every human being is called to be a unique person in communion with God and neighbor. There is only one human nature but many *hypostases*. There are a set of capacities that allow for moral decision-making. These are the ethical drive, the ethical sense, self-determination, and *mimesis*. The conscience is the hub of the moral capacities (nature) and of the situational, relational, and environmental experiences (nurture) that give morality expression. When well developed, it acts as a judge, guide, teacher, and witness. Natural law means merely the inborn human moral capacities.

The second part of this chapter spoke of evil, fallen creation, and the passions as the background of the Christian life of moral and spiritual transformation. Evil is ontologically nonexistent (*meonic*) and will someday cease to be. Evil can also be understood as failing to reach the *telos*. In terms of morality, evil is a misuse of the self-determining drive. In terms of nature, it is corruption and decay. Sin is missing the mark and, in the spiritual sense, turning away from God. The original sin of the first parents was a misuse of self-determination. The passions are triggered either by bodily needs or by relational interactions. They are caused by disharmony within the psychology of the human being, made up of belief, emotions, and desires.

The innate human capacity for imitation allows the human being to learn from models. When coupled with the human psychological powers, *mimesis* extends to desire. Human beings imitate the desire of models, which can lead to rivalry. Acquisitive mimetic desire and mimetic rivalry are essentially the nonrational psychological powers running amok. Negative *mimesis* leads to envy and aggression. Along with the self-determination drive, the original sin of the first parents was also that of modeling their desire after the wrong model (the serpent instead of God) as they attempted to circumvent God's will for them (their true *telos*) for radical self-sufficiency and autonomy (their false *telos*).

The last third of this chapter provided the remedy for negative imitation: positive *mimesis*. As a neutral innate human capacity, the ability to imitate, when presented with good models and positive objects of desire, can help the Christian overcome the individual self and be transfigured into true personhood (Christlikeness). Several Christian models were discussed at this point, but there are literally thousands of examples of Christian apostles, saints, and martyrs whose lives provide a pattern for young Christians.

Lastly, Christian parents are the first and foremost mentors in the faith to a child. How the parents live in Christ teaches the child what this faith, this life, is all about. Reading key literature to children cultivates the moral landscape and imagination like almost nothing else can, and this will be explained next. The following chapter examines the last pillar of Chrysostom's pedagogy and shows how story-telling complements and aids both imitation and the cultivation of Christian virtue.

5

Story-Telling

Threads of the Cord

FINALLY, WE REACH THE last of Chrysostom's building blocks for moral and spiritual formation in the family, story-telling. Chapter 2 touched on some of Chrysostom's thoughts on story-telling, and a brief review is in order before expanding on his views. This chapter will first discuss his perception of story-telling and its use in moral formation. Next, I will return to Alasdair MacIntyre's work on how story-telling relates to tradition and the inculcation of virtue in a community. After this, Chrysostom's thought is extended and reconceived through the modern art of the story, namely the novel. I then draw on contemporary voices in literary criticism, so that story-telling in all its various forms might be understood and used for the benefit of the Christian family. Lastly, the chapter ends with a case study of the Christian fruit of obedience and provides a guided reading of a children's novel that centers on this virtue. I take parents step by step through C. S. Lewis's *The Silver Chair* to show how Chrysostom's third element can be put into practice in nightly bedtime readings of Christ-centered stories.

ST. JOHN ON STORY-TELLING

Chrysostom viewed any story-telling to be potentially beneficial or hazardous to the moral and spiritual health of the child. Recall his metaphor of the child as a city. The various gateways into the city symbolize the child's five senses, and what comes through these gates changes the city for better or worse. Story-telling for Chrysostom was the traffic through the gates of the child's senses. Exposure to vicious gossip or gratuitous violence at the arena? Thieves and marauders breaking through the city gates. A story from Scripture or a saint's life? Good shepherds and wise sages entering the city.

Whatever kind of traveler enters the gates, each one has an impact. Perhaps this is why Chrysostom held a broad view of what constitutes a story. Stories were *anything* that had a narrative, and it was the content that made it good or bad. Thus, Chrysostom spends most of his advice using the Bible as a source for stories, but it is clear he viewed non-biblical stories also as significant. So, Chrysostom is flexible concerning stories parents choose, but he *does* discourage secular (pagan) tales if they undermine biblical truth. He gives his reason for this in a homily:

> He who seeks the doctrine of truth, shall never fall down to the earth; for that the things which are not true are of the earth, is evident from this, that all they that are without are enslaved to passions, following their own reasonings; and therefore if we are sober, we shall need no instruction in the tales of the Greeks. Do you see how weak and frivolous they are? Incapable of entertaining about God one severe thought or anything above human reasoning? Why? Because they are not *girded about with truth*.[1]

Truth as a standard for selection, then, weeds out other forms of tale-telling. In "On Vainglory," Chrysostom views gossip and old wives' tales to be a form of story-telling, along with slander. In his view, these were negative forms that were based on lies and therefore were not to be told around children. He also viewed theater, as dramatized story-telling, to be powerful. Again, content made all the difference, which is why he took such a hard-line against the theater. A parent today can find appropriate videos for the child to watch, but Chrysostom's congregation had a limited selection, and all choices were pagan. Chrysostom therefore saw nothing good about the theater, as it perpetuated lies, stirred up the passions, and presented bad models of behavior. The theater was a source of bad examples not only on the stage. The wealthy patrons as well as the social climbers used the theater to show off their lavish lifestyles with ostentatious displays of wealth. Chrysostom saw such displays as a feeding ground for vainglory.[2] As far as non-Christian stories were concerned, he urged parents to be cautious:

---

1. Chrysostom, "Homily 23," in *Homilies on Ephesians*, 164.
2. Chrysostom, "Address on Vainglory," 87–92.

> For theirs [children's childhood] is an age full of folly; and to this folly are superadded the bad examples derived from the heathen tales, where they are made acquainted with those heroes so admired among them, slaves of their passions, and cowards with regard to death; as, for example Achilles, when he relents, when he dies for his concubine, when another gets drunk, and many other things of the sort.[3]

As seen above, Chrysostom gave his congregation ample examples of the kinds of stories Christians were *not* to repeat to their young. However, he gives even more examples, both in his homilies and in "On Vainglory," of the kinds of stories the Christian *should* tell. In his preaching, he often interwove such stories through his sermons to make his point. The stories of Noah, Enoch, Elijah, Jacob, and Jonah, along with many others are referred to, sometimes very briefly, showing how familiar these biblical tales were to his congregation. In "On Vainglory," he takes great care in showing his Christian parents *how* to tell these stories. In one long passage, he takes the story of Jacob and walks parents through the entirety of Jacob's life, starting with young Jacob's rivalry with Esau. He explains what lessons might be drawn from repeated tellings of the story and how to accommodate it to the child based on age and maturity level. In one of these intervals, he says, "See how many fair lessons this story begets, and do not follow it right through to the end, but rather see how many lessons this part begets. First, children learn to reverence and honor their fathers, when they see so keen a rivalry for the father's blessing. And they will sooner suffer a myriad stripes than to hear their parents curse them. If a story can so master the children's soul that it is thought worthy of belief, the veritable truth, it will surely enthrall them and fill them with great awe."[4] He continues to move through Jacob's life, explaining the different virtues of each part, and when and how a child should hear each sequel to Jacob's story.

As shown above, Chrysostom saw stories as the content of a child's moral inner life and believed they should be used thoughtfully by Christian parents. It does not matter to him what form the story takes but whether or not it bears witness to biblical truth. To not leave his Christian parents in doubt, he guides them through an example, the multipart story of Jacob's life, stopping at various points to draw attention to moral truths revealed in the tale.

Keeping in mind Chrysostom's understanding of story-telling, the following sections below draw attention to contemporary thinkers in an effort

---

3. Chrysostom, "Homily 21," in *Homilies on Ephesians*, 154.
4. Chrysostom, "Address on Vainglory," 106.

to deepen this understanding. Chrysostom's thought will also be extended by MacIntyre's concept of tradition and the Christian family and by modern thoughts on the novel. Finally, following Chrysostom's lead, the chapter will offer its own guide through an example story taken from Christian literature, to show how biblical truths can be revealed from modern and extra-biblical sources.

TRADITION AND ITS RELATIONSHIP TO STORY-TELLING

With the preceding overview of Chrysostom's view of story-telling in mind, I now turn to a contemporary thinker's work on stories and how they affect meaning within a community. Alasdair MacIntyre agrees with Chrysostom on the importance of story, explaining that within the "classical" scheme of education, "the chief means of moral education is story-telling."[5] He explains how the Judeo-Christian, Greek and Roman, medieval and Renaissance cultures all used this method to pass on the treasury of wisdom from one generation to the next. Chrysostom testifies to this as a historical example, as he was raised in a Christian household and living in the Hellenized Roman world. Thus, it makes sense Chrysostom would see story-telling as a pillar of his pedagogical edifice, bearing an equal weight beside the pillars of spiritual exercise and imitation.

For Chrysostom, alignment with biblical truth was the standard by which a story was measured. MacIntyre acknowledges this, asserting that the stories told within a community were those that upheld the virtues of its tradition. Alasdair MacIntyre's definition of tradition is interwoven with his view of story-telling. He states: "There is no way to possess the virtues except as part of a tradition in which we inherit them and our understanding of them from a series of predecessors."[6] This understanding of the virtues is embedded in the collection of stories passed down by predecessors. If MacIntyre is correct in his assessment, then an analysis of tradition will deepen and enlarge Chrysostom's view on the nature of story-telling.

Recall Tevye's song in the musical *Fiddler on the Roof*. Tevye's life and the lives of the other villagers of Anatevka find meaning in their faith tradition. Like Anatevka, MacIntyre holds that human beings cannot escape or discard tradition. The term *tradition* has been used frequently in the above chapters, usually in terms of the Christian tradition. Christianity *is* a tradition, according to MacIntyre. It is a set of practices (virtues) habituated by

---

5. MacIntyre, *After Virtue*, 121.
6. MacIntyre, *After Virtue*, 127.

a community that enables the pursuit of a goal (*telos*) that the community shares. These practices are taught for generations by elders (like Chrysostom) to the young by example and through the telling of the tradition's stock of stories, legends, and myths. For the Christian community (the church), the goal is the kingdom of God. The Bible, the lives of saints and martyrs, and Christian literature are the shared stories told and read repeatedly by the members of the community.

As MacIntyre states, there is no "neutral independent ground" upon which to stand, no society or community free from tradition.[7] Even anti-tradition ideologies are part of a tradition. At its core, tradition is an argument, conversation, or inquiry a community has with itself over time, on what constitutes the good or, rather, what constitutes the purpose of life. Tradition, in other words, is a shared quest for the best way of life. Different living traditions—and a tradition *is* alive if it continues, after generations, to pursue the argument of the good—answer the question of what is "the good" differently. How a tradition is socially embodied by the community that argues for and pursues the good determines the catalogue of virtues that are upheld, taught, and lived out. Thus, a tradition is multidimensional and can be described or manifested in different ways. Some of these ways will be discussed below, but first is a presentation of alternatives to tradition.

Tradition and Its Rivals

Tradition must be explained, because St. John Chrysostom held the classical, premodern view of knowledge. As MacIntyre points out, tradition *was* the conveyer of knowledge for the ancients. As discussed in chapter 1, however, there are now alternatives to this viewpoint. The two competing perspectives that reject the concept of tradition were born from the Enlightenment. One view holds that there is a universal framework for all knowledge, and this framework is in the realm of empirical science. Morality is perceived as a natural science. MacIntyre calls this the encyclopedic framework. "The central presupposition" of this standpoint is that "on questions of standards, criteria, and method all rational persons can resolve their disagreements."[8] This leads MacIntyre to ask, which rationality? The main proponents of the encyclopedic framework were eighteenth- to nineteenth-century European men who were blinded by their bias, which made them unable to see how other people in other cultures in other places might not share their same "rationality." Despite this flaw, the encyclopedic viewpoint remains

7. MacIntyre, *Whose Justice*, 346.
8. MacIntyre, *Three Rival Versions*, 170.

influential, especially within the academic institution in the modern curriculum, as knowledge, as it is presented, is divided and compartmentalized by discipline.

The second alternative to tradition was fathered by Nietzsche and is called the genealogical framework. It is fundamentally opposed to the realism of Judeo-Christian theism. The moral genealogist believes truth is

> a mobile army of metaphors, metonymies, anthropomorphisms, a sum, in short, of human relationships which, rhetorically and poetically intensified, ornamented and transformed, come to be thought of, after long usage by a people, as fixed, binding, and canonical. Truths are illusions which we have forgotten are illusions, worn-out metaphors now impotent to stir the senses, coins which have lost their faces and are considered now as metal rather than currency.[9]

The moral relativity of this viewpoint makes it untenable to the Christian. The Christian upholds the belief in (biblical) tradition as the source of knowledge, because Christian theism is realistic and perfectionist. Truth is real, and the faith is essentially concerned with truth. Many others seek to be religious because it "works," or it helps them have a meaningful life and reconciles them with dying. Even secularism is a religion by this standard. The great liturgical theologian Alexander Schmemann writes concerning secularism as a faith, "If 'help' were the criterion, one would have to admit that life-centered secularism *helps* actually more than religion. To compete with it, religion must present itself as 'adjustment to life,' 'counseling,' 'enrichment,' and so on." As he saw it, the difference between Christianity and all other alternatives is that, for the Christian,

> *help* is not the criterion. Truth is the criterion. The purpose of Christianity is not to help people by reconciling them with death, but to reveal the Truth about life and death in order that people may be saved by this Truth. Salvation, however, is not only not identical to help, but is, in fact, opposed to it . . . . Christianity is not reconciliation with death. It is the revelation of death, and it reveals death because it is the revelation of Life. Christ is this Life. And only if Christ is Life is death what Christianity proclaims it to be, namely the enemy to be destroyed, and not a "mystery" to be explained.[10]

---

9. Nietzsche, as quoted in MacIntyre, *Three Rival Versions*, 35.
10. Schmemann, *For the Life*, 119–20.

Both the encyclopedic and the genealogical viewpoints leave faith behind or, at the very least, put faith subservient to rationality. The world is narrowed, demystified, and "demythologized," and the human being is reduced to the material realm.

Tradition as *Techne*

Techne is the ancient Greek word for work or craft. The classical perspective is that a tradition is like a craft. Every craft has an end in mind (the *telos*), and so does tradition. The master of a craft teaches his apprentice the art and skill, the best practices and standards, and then it is up to the pupil to perfect this knowledge and become a master craftsman or craftswoman. Every now and then, a prodigy will spring up, granting the craft a new best standard, and the craft continues, refined and handed down to generations of craftsmen and craftswomen. The Christian faith, at its very core, shares this view of reality. The ultimate master is Jesus Christ, and his disciples all seek to be like the master, work like the master, and carry out the master's will. Every now and then, a prodigy of the faith emerges, and that voice becomes a secondary authority to the master's, but only because the example and teachings are so like his.

Tradition as the Historical Dimension of Virtue

Thus, practices (virtues) do not spring from thin air. Generally speaking, a set of practices is developed by the historical needs of a society. In this sense, tradition is also a relationship, one as equally embedded in time and space as any other relationship. Tradition is the connection of the virtues to the past. When I enter into a tradition, I am immediately in a relationship with the other practitioners of faith or the craft (as in medical practice)—not only with living members but with those practitioners of the past whose deeds or contributions continue to influence the present. The fact that this book centers on the work of Chrysostom is a good example of this concept. Chrysostom was a "practitioner" of the past whose work is influencing the present by this current conversation.

Another aspect of the historical dimension of tradition is the creation of institutions. As MacIntyre points out, practices are not the same thing as institutions, but many practices are sustained by institutions in order to survive.[11] Sometimes, a tradition is an institution as well. This is the case of

---

11. MacIntyre, *After Virtue*, 194.

universities and academies that began as scholarly traditions that became institutionalized. Think of Aristotle's view of philosophy as a *techne* that can be mastered, honed, and taught to new disciples. Almost every institution started out as a simple tradition.

Only when a tradition loses its practitioners, through the devaluation of what was once considered the virtues of the community, does a tradition start to die. Without the practice of its core virtues, the tradition becomes a thing of the past, a memory of a way of life that is gone, no longer relevant to the here and now. The stories told have long been forgotten and are not retold to every new child of the community. In a way, the tradition lives only if the stories are told and are alive in the imaginations of the hearers.

As an ongoing argument, we should not be surprised that traditions always hold within themselves a certain amount of conflict. If the bearers of tradition stop questioning, questing, and arguing for the *telos*, then it is because the tradition stopped being relevant. Again, when the stories stop being told, the virtues of the irrelevant tradition are lost and ignored, and cultivation is discontinued. The practitioners have found their quest, questions, and arguments in another tradition, or a new tradition has been formed.

Tradition as Community

Return to the social aspect of tradition. In his extension of MacIntyre's thought, Stanley Hauweras spills a good deal of ink speaking of tradition as community. In his book *A Community of Character*, he uses the allegorical children's story *Watership Down* to show how the community exemplifies the tradition through its stories and the virtues appropriated by the community members. Tradition, as a community, is viewed by Hauerwas and MacIntyre as "story-formed."[12] This idea of the story-shaped tradition is echoed by Christos Yannaras when Yannaras calls the Christian pursuit of God an adventure.[13] All adventures have a beginning, middle, and end, just like the story. They all have their heroes, the main protagonist of the story, and many supporting characters to guide and mentor the hero through pitfalls and treachery. And there is always an adversary, a great enemy who encounters the hero or sends his representatives to snare the hero. The archetypal story is the basis for Joseph Campbell's classic, *The Hero with a Thousand*

---

12. Hauerwas, *Community of Character*, 9.

13. "What we call the *morality* of man is the way he relates to this adventure of his freedom" (Yannaras, *Freedom of Morality*, 24).

Faces, which was so influential that it found its way into popular culture and inspired George Lucas's *Star Wars* series.

A tradition, with its stories, becomes part of one's identity, one's character.[14] "What I am, therefore, is in key part what I inherit, a specific past that is present to some degree in my present. I find myself part of a history that is generally to say, whether I like it or not, whether I recognize it or not, one of the bearers of a tradition."[15] Life is unintelligible if it is not situated within a story. For the Christian, the witness of the gospel is "the greatest story ever told," and the identity of the believer is shaped by the Christian community.

I was once chided by a teacher because I could quote whole sections of the Bible, but I rarely could tell him the chapter and verse I was quoting. He considered it a lack of spiritual discipline on my part. Viewed in light of tradition, however, I would say that my life is so formed by the "story" of Scripture that I can recite passages the way some can recite their favorite books or movies. In my defense, the ancient practitioners of the Christian faith did this as well. The writers of the New Testament liberally paraphrased and quoted their Bible (the Hebrew Old Testament) throughout their writings. They knew their Bible by heart, and it shaped their lives and the new story (the gospel) that they were writing.

Christianity as Tradition

If MacIntyre is correct, that traditions rely on the virtues habituated by adherents who furthermore learn these virtues through the stock stories told from one generation to the next, then Chrysostom's belief in story-telling as a key element to moral education is confirmed to a great degree by contemporary thinkers. Likewise, these same contemporary thinkers are thinking along the same lines as Chrysostom, whether or not they have actually encountered his work. Yet tradition is more than just its stories. For example, Lossky defines Christian tradition as mystical theology:

> Now tradition is not merely the aggregate of dogmas, of sacred institutions, and of rites which the Church preserves. It is, above all, that which expresses in its outward determinations a living tradition, the unceasing revelation of the Holy Spirit in the Church; a life in which each one of her members can share according to his capacity. To be in the tradition is to share in the experience of mysteries revealed to the Church. Doctrinal

---

14. See Hauerwas, *Community of Character*.
15. MacIntyre, *After Virtue*, 221.

tradition—beacons set up by the Church along the channel of the knowledge of God—cannot be separated from or opposed to mystical tradition: acquired experience of the mysteries of the faith. Dogma cannot be understood apart from experience; the fullness of experience cannot be had apart from true doctrine . . . mystical theology—doctrine and experience mutually conditioning each other.[16]

Tradition in this expanded definition includes elements pointed out by MacIntyre. It is a community of members that receives the wisdom passed down from the earliest church and incorporates it in its beliefs. The disciplines of the church, the spiritual practices, are learned and crafted to mastery, with an eye to the cultivation of those practices (the fruit of the Spirit) that move the disciple closer to the *telos* of the tradition. Tradition is historical and present, experiential as well as taught, living and lived out. A unique mark of the Christian tradition is the belief in the church as "theandric," that it was literally instituted by the Holy Spirit at Pentecost (Acts 2) and is truly an institution created by God. This expanded sense of tradition means that Chrysostom would never put all the responsibility of moral education on story-telling. The spiritual exercises are possible only through God's grace, and the imitation of Spirit-filled mentors is undeniably a part of the life of faith. Yet story-telling can also be a Spirit-led and Spirit-filled process, which is why it is one of the threads of Chrysostom's golden cord.

THE MODERN NOVEL AS A CONTINUATION OF CHRISTIAN STORY-TELLING

I now will build on Chrysostom's idea of the story. Again, Chrysostom held a broad understanding of what made a story. As long as it was a narrative, it could take many forms, including folktales, epic poetry, drama, and gossip. The novel as it is known in modernity did not exist in Chrysostom's day, but it fits well within the parameter he laid down. Just as he discussed various forms of the story in his day, it is helpful to examine the novel to see how it fits within his concept of story-telling.

I begin this discussion of the novel with the origin of the story itself. Story-telling has been a part of human life from the beginning. Every family, tribe, and civilization has told stories in oral tradition. Although oral tradition is sometimes thought of as a primitive method of recordkeeping, every family uses this method, as grandparents tell their grandchildren

---

16. Lossky, *Mystical Theology*, 236.

about their childhood, hoping the family's identity and tradition will be remembered and retained when they are gone. Elders have long been the cultural gatekeepers of the family. Despite this, the earliest writings found by archaeologists are banal—cuneiform tablets used as receipts for trade goods. Yet with the invention of written language, other records were soon written down, including origin stories, epic poetry, fables, proverbs, and revelations from God. An innovation in writing came rather late in human history, as the emergence of modernity brought a new way of writing, the *roman* style, which suited the needs of the age. The premodern age used its own distinct form of story-telling:

> *Chanson* fiction (tales of ideal types performing symbolically charged actions, without much revealed interior self) is more than adequate, perhaps even preferable, for stories told in a world thick with supernatural realities. What we called *roman* fiction (accounts of characters with internal processes and psychological identity) becomes necessary when we wish to present human figures as something real within themselves.[17]

This great artistic invention of modernity was the novel. The novel was meant to speak truth to the era. Novel reading became "the great hunt into the human condition akin to (or, at least, providing the raw material for) serious intellectual analysis of ethics, political theory, and psychology."[18] Novel writing was story-telling as an art form, and the stories encapsulated metaphysical truths that could not be easily digested any other way. This was a distinctly Christian art form, as the novelist's very purpose was to chart the interior world of the self as the self pursued sanctification. "The novel came into being to present the Protestant story of the individual soul as it strove to understand its salvation and achieve its sanctification, illustrated by the parallel journey of the new-style characters, with their well-furnished interiors, as they wandered through their adventures in the exterior world."[19] The novel was born in the aftermath of the Protestant Reformation and was further developed through the Renaissance and the Enlightenment. Most literary specialists mark Miguel Cervantes's *Don Quixote* of 1605 as the beginning of the modern novel. There have been other, premodern contenders for this title, however, including Apuleius's *Golden Ass*, Murasaki Shikibu's *Tale of Genji* (c. 1020), and China's *Romance of the Three Kingdoms* (c. 1500). Although these were all lengthy works of prose, in *Don Quixote* we have the novel as epitomized in this chapter. By the nineteenth

---

17. Bottum, *Decline of the Novel*, 48.
18. Bottum, *Decline of the Novel*, 5.
19. Bottum, *Decline of the Novel*, 11–12.

century, some of the greatest novels of all time were written. The reason for the novel's development during this transitory time (from premodern to modern) is believed to have been a result of the "modern crisis of the self."[20] The spiritual realm was now interiorized in the self, as the external world, once dense with supernatural meaning, was emptied of transcendent reality.

The Enlightenment did its part during this process of modernization, as the idea of a natural human purpose was rejected. The joining together of new, scientific thinking; the innovative drive of the Industrial Revolution; the rise of democracy in the West, along with the nation-state; the emergence of bureaucracies; and common sense rationalism all had a part in the making of the modern novel into a dominant art form. The novelist represented the new modern individual, who struggled in a world emptied of its spiritual and metaphysical thickness. "What saints and demons, angels and devils, ghosts and monsters were to people in the Middle Ages, the self became to moderns: an object of metaphysical weight in the secular world greater than anything ever contemplated before."[21] Indeed, the novel was meant to retain some of that thickness, if only within the interior world of the individual soul, a sort of re-enchantment of the world lost by the advent of modernity.

Yet, the novel failed. Joseph Bottum, in his book *The Decline of the Novel*, sees the emergence of this art form as "the canary in the coal mine," as the last gasp of a dying tradition. He argues that the novel failed and has been rendered nearly dead in importance. Modern society has looked elsewhere for a sense of supernatural density, for the re-enchantment of the world, turning to spiritualism and the occult, astrology, and theosophy. No one reads or writes great novels anymore. Indeed, the classic novel, once written for an adult audience, is now considered children's literature, as though books about truth, good and evil, and the human condition are only suitable for the young, for those who have not matured to the suitable age of nihilism. At the peak of the novel's art form, children's novels were invented. Before the Victorians, there were no books written specifically for children. This might be why today's popular children's fiction yet retains some of the novelistic strain, the original purpose repackaged, as if "to put great clashes of good and evil without irony, if to use the ideas of virtue and vice with serious intent, if to show the world-changing journey as instancing a soul-changing transformation, we have to go to books aimed at the young."[22]

---

20. Bottum, *Decline of the Novel*, 47.
21. Bottum, *Decline of the Novel*, 48.
22. Bottum, *Decline of the Novel*, 128.

In his article "Books about Next to Nothing," John Waters comments about the current state of the novel. Today's novel writers have lost the key component to what constitutes a novel: the ability to speak truth concerning human existence. Instead, the current novels seem to be, indeed, books about next to nothing, like *Seinfeld* episodes. As Waters puts it poignantly,

> In abolishing God, man obscured mystery, including the mystery of himself. Marooned in his self-created world-without-wonder, hunchbacked by the low ceilings he had installed above his own head, he became more convinced of his growing intelligence, until his imagination shrank and dried up. His story, incapable of achieving a lucid ending, stuttered to a halt.[23]

This is the individual disconnected from his story and tradition, alienated from God and neighbor.

Despite the novel's slow death, I draw attention to its original purpose for a reason. Remember, the novel was written to speak truth to its generation, and Chrysostom understood the key aspect of the right story to be its ability to affirm biblical truth. Regardless of Western civilization's overall state of health, Christianity is still a living tradition that has produced a precious treasure trove of stories in novel form, all of which fit Chrysostom's standard of truth-bearing. These jewels can continue to be read to shape and transform the lives of the reader or listener. A reader of the classic novel absorbs the story, it becomes part of the reader, living within the interior world of the mind, just as Chrysostom conveyed in his metaphor of the city.

Although no new novels (in their classical sense) are being written, the novels of the last three centuries are still available for the Christian family to read aloud during story-time. A book found lovable by the father and mother and read at bedtime will leave its mark on the child. There are so many wonderful novels that parents can pick and choose based on age-appropriateness, and they, as well as their children, can grow up spiritually with increasingly mature stories. If traditions are story-shaped, then the novel complements the Bible in forming the moral landscape of the child's inner mind. Parents are not immune to the effects of the novel either and are refortified spiritually through the reading of the great Christian art form.

As for newer popular fiction, Bottum points out that other genres, including the graphic novel,[24] have absorbed much of what the novel once was. These books are not written for the sole purpose of the sanctification of the reader, but they do take on some of the main themes present in the

---

23. Waters, "Books about Next to Nothing."

24. Bottum remarks that Neil Gaiman's *Sandman* comic book series is filled with novelistic characteristics and themes.

classics. Chosen with care, parents can mix some new with the old, to create a veritable garden of stories in the imagination of the child.

THE NOVEL AS STORY TESTIFYING TO TRUTH

I now will attempt innovation. I will marry Chrysostom's view of the story (and the novel as a story, by his broad definition) with René Girard's observations. Girard saw the distinctive quality of the novel as he taught European literature early in his career as a professor at Johns Hopkins University. Like Joseph Bottum, he perceived the great novelist as a bearer of truth, who exposes the warp and weft of human relationships, the falseness of individualism, and who ultimately struggles with the world emptied of spiritual transcendence. He found that "literature accurately described human relationships long before psychology, anthropology and sociology were established as academic disciplines."[25] Indeed, what Girard discovered in literature was the genesis of his major theory on imitation and culture discussed in the previous chapter. He calls the phenomenological insight within these works "novelistic knowledge."

Just as Chrysostom saw truth as a necessary element to the right kind of story, Girard believed novelistic knowledge bore witness to ultimate truth, making it naturally opposed to both the reductionism of the encyclopedists and the denial of truth by the moral genealogist. Girard's theory can be presented through these alternatives, as Girard borrows from both encyclopedic thinkers like Frazier and Freud and genealogical thinkers like Hegel, Sartre, and Kojève. He had to be both knowledgeable and deft to navigate and critique these waters. In the end, he maintained that novelists, playwrights, and poets had "a deeper insight into the structure of identity and desire than philosophers, critics, or analysts."[26] In this way, Girard is a heavyweight intellectual whose writings on myth and literature give many Christians and scholars a powerful defense against the heroes of modernity listed in chapter 1—Hume, Descartes, Nietzsche, Sartre, Fletcher, and many other proponents of the alternatives to tradition.

Girard's concept of "novelistic knowledge" that reveals triangular (mimetic) desire and the "novelistic conversion" were discussed in the previous chapter, yet now these concepts must be framed within Chrysostom's view of story-telling as a pillar of moral education. Girard's system of literary analysis was "to interrogate a series of texts . . . in order to see what they

---

25. Girard, as quoted in Antonello and Webb, *Mimesis, Desire*, xii.
26. Antonello and Webb, *Mimesis, Desire*, xviii.

have to say about human relationship."[27] For example, in his work of literary criticism on Dostoyevsky's novels, *Resurrection from the Underground*, he states, "It is not the disincarnate thought that interests us but the thought embodied in the novels."[28] The complexity of human nature unfolds even in current children's literature. Parents can learn from Girard's efforts how to "interrogate" children's books with their kids by ending each chapter with a lively conversation. As shown above with his example of Jacob, Chrysostom describes a similar sort of guided interrogation of the biblical story by parents of their children through repeated recitation of Bible stories.

Two contemporary examples of such interrogations can be found in popular book series written in the twenty-first-century. These examples are provided by Jennifer Garcia Bashaw in her essay "Jesus, Girard, and Dystopian Literature," as Bashaw analyzes the *Hunger Games* trilogy and *Divergent* series through the overlay of mimetic theory in order to offer insight into human interaction and social behaviors. Both popular series of books are dystopian science fiction written for a young adult audience. To reinforce Joseph Bottum's assertion that today's popular genre fiction is the natural offspring of the novel, note that anti-utopian literature was born with Fyodor Dostoevsky's *Notes from Underground*. Bashaw exposes the destructive pattern of human behavior through the characters and events of these stories, revealing how fiction can shed light on the mysteries of human behavior for the young adults reading these books. This is an element of the classical scheme, a part of the novel that lives on in genre fiction. The right kind of book—whether it be a classic novel or new popular fiction that contains these novelistic elements—is a work of art meant to be enjoyed as it transforms the reader/listener. "To read well is not to scour books for lessons on *what* to think. Rather, to read well is to be formed in *how* to think."[29]

Another revealing essay on children's literature is Melody Green's "Jesus, Girard, and Twentieth-Century Fantasy for Young Adults." Green digs through two post-WWII children's books to uncover biblical truth and themes using Girard's theory of violence. She writes, "In this essay, I focus on two such narratives, *The Perilous Gard* and *The Black Cauldron*, both of which feature scapegoats that are reminiscent of the Christ figure, whose 'deaths' mark the endpoint of the communal custom of ritual sacrifice." These narratives, which can be read as allegories of the passion, like their more famous brethren, *The Chronicles of Narnia*, invariably inculcate Christian concepts within the young reader. With just a little bit of knowledge

---

27. Antonello and Webb, *Mimesis, Desire*, xii.
28. Girard, as quoted in Antonello and Webb, *Mimesis, Desire*, xii.
29. Prior, *On Reading Well*, 18.

and practice, the family can enjoy these stories together and gain deeper insight in biblical truth.

THE STORY AS A TRAINING GROUND FOR VICARIOUS VIRTUE

Another contemporary thinker, Karen Swallow Prior, reflects a view on story-telling similar to Chrysostom's. She sees stories as having significant benefits in terms of moral development, as, for example, the cultivation of empathy in readers who are cognitively making value judgments as they follow the story, which helps them to make the same kind of judgments later in everyday life. As Prior points out in her essay "The Art of Virtuous Reading," everyone reads now. She relates how, at the beginning of her career as a college literature professor, she struggled to get her young college students to read, to simply expose them to another world. Now she has a new problem. Everyone reads constantly, she finds, but they are not *reading well*. She has had to become an evangelist for classic literature, because the devolution of the written word, combined with the influx of reading material, has coincided with a lack of empathy, as can be seen on any internet forum. Indeed, she calls this a "post-literate age."[30] It is telling indeed that the time of the "post-literate" coincides with the era of moral ambiguity, but that is a topic for another book.

Prior picks up the theme of her essay in her book *On Reading Well* and gives a defense for the power of good stories and story-telling. In her preface, she begins by pointing out that both pagan and Christian sources saw literature as useful for moral development, which agrees with MacIntyre's argument at the beginning of this chapter. Aristotle saw that good literature "satisfies the moral sense."[31] Christian Renaissance author Sir Philip Sidney agrees with this sentiment in his *Defense of Poetry*, claiming Joseph Bottum's same argument, that literature is meant for the "winning of the mind from wickedness to virtue."[32]

Prior's main argument agrees with our previous thinkers on how literature helps moral and spiritual transformation. Her book explores what reading well accomplishes, cognitively, aesthetically, and in moral formation. Simply reading a novel deeply is described by Prior as a practice in perseverance. She points to current research in neuroscience describing

---

30. See Prior, "Art of Virtuous Reading."
31. Aristotle, as quoted in Prior, *On Reading Well*, 9.
32. Philip Sidney, as quoted in Prior, *On Reading Well*, 9.

the effects of reading on the internet and how it affects the brain's attention span. Reading a novel creates an orderly mind:

> To read virtuously is to rebel against this chaos. Above all, reading well requires reading closely: being faithful to both text and context, interpreting accurately and insightfully. The attentiveness necessary for deep reading—the kind we practice in reading literary works as opposed to skimming news stories or social media posts—requires patience. Careful interpretation and evaluation require prudence. To practice any of these skills is to cultivate the virtues they demand.[33]

Although the cognitive and aesthetic benefits of reading well are greatly beneficial, it is Prior's discussion of virtue that I find most helpful. The cultivating of virtue through literature, Prior asserts, is due to "vicarious practice." She explains, "Literature embodies virtue, first, by offering images of virtue in action and second, by offering the reader vicarious practice in exercising virtue, which is not the same as actual practice, of course, but is nonetheless a practice by which habits of mind, ways of thinking and perceiving, accrue."[34] As the reader comes to identify with the character of a story, she not only learns about human nature but about her own humanity as she undergoes the adventure of the plot, living vicariously through the character's experience. "In other words, plot reveals character. And the act of judging the character of a character shapes the reader's own character."[35]

The novel's parallel world is a mirror of the real world, and learning occurs through the imagination in a similar way as happens outside of the mind.[36] In her essay, Prior illustrates how this happens: "In portraying virtue (and vice) in action, great works of literature provide vicarious experience in exercising virtue or bearing the consequences of vice . . . . The process of evaluating characters in literature—good, bad, or a mixture of both, like most everyone in life—is a process that shapes our own character. It is a virtue-building enterprise."[37]

Vicarious experience, as a quality of literature, is why Prior makes *The History of Tom Jones, a Foundling* a required book in her classes. She calls

---

33. Prior, "Art of Virtuous Reading," 36.
34. Prior, *On Reading Well*, 15.
35. Prior, *On Reading Well*, 20.
36. To clarify, "the moral imagination is not a *thing*, not even so much a faculty, as the very process by which the self makes metaphors out of images given by experience and then employs these metaphors to find and suppose moral correspondence in experience" (Guroian, *Tending the Heart*, 24).
37. Prior, "Art of Virtuous Reading," 36–37.

the work a "veritable school of virtue ethics"[38] and notes that Henry Fielding, in his dedication, explains his purpose:

> To recommend goodness and innocence hath been my sincere endeavor in this history. This honest purpose you have been pleased to think I have attained: and to say the truth, it is likeliest to be attained in books of this kind; for an example is a kind of picture, in which virtue becomes, as it were, an object of sight, and strikes us with an idea of that loveliness, which Plato asserts there is in her naked charms.
>
> Besides displaying that beauty of virtue which may attract the admiration of mankind, I have attempted to engage a stronger motive to human action in her favour, by convincing men that their true interest directs them to a pursuit of her.

Fielding's purpose and Prior's thesis align with Girard's view of literature. Fielding is offering up an external mediator, a character one can identify with and appropriate, whose object of desire ("an object of sight") is virtue. Knowing the power of imitation, Fielding is presenting a model for the reader to desire. This is vicarious practice of virtue based on a fictional model.

Another virtue cultivated by the reading of novels is attentiveness. Attentiveness requires the reader or listener to focus on the words for a sustained period. This cultivation of attention, or mindfulness, is the same as needed in prayer.[39] Prior even goes so far as to state, "Reading is inherently virtuous. Consider the fact that Christianity is a religion of the word, a faith centered on words and, ultimately, the Word itself."[40]

TENDING THE GARDEN OF THE IMAGINATION

Basing much of his research on Chrysostom's homilies and even "On Vainglory," theologian Vigen Guroian likens the imagination of a child not to a city but to a garden. The garden, when cared for diligently and lovingly, bears the fruit of the Spirit. In his inspiring book on children's stories, Guroian remarks that the clearest indicator the human being is naturally endowed with a moral constitution is reading to a child and hearing the refrain, "But is he good or bad?" or "Is she a good fairy or a bad one?"[41] A common phrase

---

38. Prior, *On Reading Well*, 37.

39. David Marno chronicles Christian history and literature on the cultivation of this virtue through spiritual practice (see Marno, *Death Be Not Proud*).

40. Prior, "Art of Virtuous Reading."

41. Guroian, *Tending the Heart*, 4.

is "children want boundaries." This is especially true of moral boundaries, as children thirst for moral clarity. This desire can be both irritating and uncomfortable for parents who feel unequipped or unworthy of providing this clarity. Guroian describes this problem based on his experience as a father and teacher, explaining how daunting a responsibility it is to be the main educator of morality to a child. Yet this is a task that remains a responsibility of the parent, no matter to whom he tries to delegate it. I have heard a common lament among Christian parents who see their children reject their (the parents') faith. "I don't know what happened. They grew up in the church!" or "They went to Sunday school!"—as if having once placed the child at the appropriate venue, the task of moral and spiritual formation was complete. This shows a propensity to buy into the belief that someone else is a better teacher or "expert" and to distrust one's own capacity for mentorship.

As a mother of young children, I sympathize with these parents and hold a deep fear that I, too, will experience the loss of a child to the moral dystopia of our age. Why else would I spend so much time trying to find an answer to the perennial question of how to raise godly children? On the first page of his book, Guroian comes right to the crux of the issue:

> Our society is finding it difficult to meet these needs of children. Some well-meaning educators and parents seem to want to drive the passion for moral clarity out of children rather than use it to the advantage of shaping their character. We want our children to be tolerant, and we sometimes seem to think that a too sure sense of right and wrong only produces fanatics. Perhaps we have become so resigned to flailing about in the culture's muddy waters of moral compromise and ethical obscurantism that it is hard for us to imagine other possibilities for our children. I am no exception. And sometimes I also find myself doing what I often criticize in others, nervously rationalizing my laziness or unwillingness to cultivate conscience and moral sense in my own children. Mostly we fall back on the excuse that we are respecting our children's freedom by permitting them to determine right from wrong and to choose for themselves clear goals of moral living. But this is the paean of a false freedom that pays misdirected tribute to a deeply flawed notion of individual autonomy. We end up forfeiting our parental authority and failing to be mentors to our children in the moral life.[42]

---

42. Guroian, *Tending the Heart*, 3–4.

If this sounds familiar, recall the first chapter's discussion on the state of moral failure in which our culture finds itself. It is almost inconceivable that parents would *not* find themselves at a loss, even Christian parents who have the biblical ethic on which to build. This sense of incompetence is compounded by a society that views parents more like administrators of their child's life, who set up the child's day to be structured by "experts" who will take on a series of roles that were once solely in the domain of the parents. This places most of the child's time in the hands of others, and especially in the "benign hands of the state and school."[43] Yet it is family life that gives the child his origin story, his starting place in time, situated within a tradition shaped by these people, in this culture, in this ethnicity, etc. The family is thus story-shaped, too, with a historical sense and linear chronology.

The moral shaping of children happens regardless, as children take their cues from the parents' behavior. To expect children to decide what is right or wrong independently is like asking them to create their own language, or to develop their own mathematical system. "These [value-clarification] educators think that moral education is like teaching children reading or arithmetic.... Yet we do not permit children to invent their own math: we teach them the multiplication tables; nor do we encourage children to make up their own personal alphabet: we teach them how to read."[44] It is a ridiculous demand and an excuse driven by the belief in a radical individualism that is at odds with biblical teaching. Like Chrysostom, Guroian offers a literary guide to parents, pointing to key children's fairy tales and novels that will naturally teach the child to decipher metaphor, a key part of the moral language. While story-telling is only one of several elements for spiritual and moral maturity, it is necessary. Just as the child is growing, the parents grow, too, as both are exercising moral muscles through this shared time together, unified as a family—and unity is a mark of the church, including the "little church."

C. S. Lewis and the Art of Story-Telling

It is fitting to end a discussion about story-telling with the thoughts of a master story-teller. C. S. Lewis was a professor of literature, a theologian, and an author. His children's books, *The Chronicles of Narnia*, are upheld by Guroian as the kind of literature that inculcates virtue in the young reader. Prior discusses Lewis's thought from his essay "An Experiment in Criticism," and Joseph Bottom calls Lewis the father of a "silver age" in great children's

---

43. Hauerwas, *Community of Character*, 158–66.
44. Guroian, *Tending the Heart*, 34.

literature. Suffice it to say, Lewis belongs in this discussion as surely as Alasdair MacIntyre, for he is a notable proponent for tradition. Indeed, Lewis's book *The Abolition of Man* provides a keen (and certainly more readable) defense against emotivism than what is presented in *After Virtue*, making it ideal for a wider audience.

Prior mentioned that we live in a "post-literate" age. If this is so, what does it mean to be literate? Lewis gives us the answer in *An Experiment in Criticism*. He argues that, out of many readers, there have always been only a few who are literate. He obviously does not mean literate in the technical sense of the ability to read but more as Prior means, to be able to read with *depth*. To explain the literate, he delves into art and music, both experienced in ways parallel to the art of literature. When we truly see a work of great art, "we sit down before the picture in order to have something done to us, not that we may do things with it. The first demand of any work of any art makes upon us is surrender. Look. Listen. Receive. Get yourself out of the way. (There is no good in asking first whether the work before you deserves such a surrender, for until you have surrendered you cannot possibly find out)."[45] Here, Lewis sees great art as objects of beauty that give glimpses of the divine Source. The quasi-religious tones fit with the understanding of the novel, created for the spiritual formation of the writer and reader. "The first reading of some literary work is often, to the literary, an experience so momentous that only experiences of love, religion, or bereavement can furnish a standard of comparison. Their whole consciousness is changed. They have become what they were not before."[46]

Perhaps the best illustration of what Lewis means by the literary person is given by his example of the teddy bear or the religious icon. The stuffed toy is created with the purpose of being a blank canvas for the imagination. The child can "endow it with imaginary life and personality and enter into a quasi-social relationship with it. That is what 'playing with it' means."[47] The sacred icon is created with a similar purpose in mind. It is not a vehicle or object to use but a way to pass "through the material image and go beyond" into a higher reality. Great stories have this purpose, Lewis understands. They are not to be used as an escape, to pass the time and then forget or to teach the reader a lesson. The novel is instead meant to change the reader as she interacts with the character and landscape, living vicariously through them.

---

45. Lewis, *Experiment in Criticism*, 19.
46. Lewis, *Experiment in Criticism*, 3.
47. Lewis, *Experiment in Criticism*, 17.

The teddy bear and the sacred icon are not identical in the way they work with those who encounter them. Yet they both, like the great piece of art, are the means by which we enter into a relationship that changes us inwardly, instead of outwardly through the intellect. Sanctification is not an intellectual exercise but an experiential relationship with the God who is both transcendent and immanent. We cannot know him by reading a textbook but by meeting him through the heart, by way of the chest. The teddy bear, the icon, and the beauty embodied in the masterpiece all reach us through the heart.

Perhaps Lewis makes a better case for the purpose of literature in education in his book *The Abolition of Man*. He states that "the task of the modern educator is not to cut down jungles but to irrigate deserts."[48] The desert is the child's imagination, which is being starved to death, in Lewis's view, by educators who, with the best intentions, are erasing any sensitivity to objective truth within their students on the grounds of rationality.

Moral educators are in two camps. One camp is filled with those holding David Hume's view of the world, with its reduction to the material, with human beings subjected to and enslaved by their emotions. This is the anti-tradition camp, for it not only emphasizes empirical data and rationality, but it denies any existence of objective truth. The second camp is that of tradition, which embodies what Lewis describes as the *Tao*. The *Tao* is "the reality beyond all predicates.... It is Nature, it is the Way, the Road."[49] Lewis provides another explanation: "It is the doctrine of objective value, the belief that certain attitudes are really true, and others really false, to the kind of thing the universe is and the kind of things we are.... [The *Tao*] demands a certain response from us whether we make it or not."[50]

If the *Tao* is the true way and the way of the universe, then the heart, as the seat of emotions, must be cultivated and trained to be sensitive to the way. The one who embraces the *Tao* has the opposite understanding of human nature to Hume, as "the heart never takes the place of the head: but it can, and should, obey it."[51] Lewis further states, "Without the aid of trained emotions the intellect is powerless against the animal organism."[52] Story-telling, in this sense, is the irrigation placed in the desert. Guroian makes a similar statement, stating that the moral imagination "is active, for well or ill, strongly or weakly, every moment of our lives... it needs nurture

48. Lewis, *Abolition of Man*, 13–14.
49. Lewis, *Abolition of Man*, 18.
50. Lewis, *Abolition of Man*, 18–19.
51. Lewis, *Abolition of Man*, 19.
52. Lewis, *Abolition of Man*, 24.

and proper exercise. Otherwise, it will atrophy like a muscle that is not used. The richness or poverty of the moral imagination depends on the richness or poverty of experience."[53] Likewise, Prior speaks of the importance of literature in providing vicarious experience. The better (in terms of moral richness) the story, the better experience to exercise the inner mind. "The head rules the belly through the chest," as the heart is the seat "of emotions organized by trained habit into stable sentiments."[54] A child's heart is trained by the tending of the garden, the oasis that springs up in the desert of the imagination.

Chrysostom likened the child's mind to a city that must be guarded and ruled by a good monarch, one who lets the right people in—the traders and craftsmen, the farmers coming to market, the traveler passing through—and keeps the wrong people out—the bandits, rogues, and murderers who would tear the city apart. In Guroian's metaphor, the garden must be weeded and the crop-eating insects destroyed. Lewis would simply have us gift our sons and daughters with *Treasure Island* or *The Princess and the Goblin* and leave Garth Nix's *Angel Mage* at the bookstore.

I wish to pause for a moment and consider the current state of young adult publishing. Nix is a good example of what parents might find when looking for literature for their older and middle-school-aged children. He is a contemporary children's fantasy author whose late twentieth-century works, particularly the *Old Kingdom* series, retain many themes of the classical novel. However, his latest work is empty of these elements. Instead of heroines and heroes who epitomize courage and perseverance, his new protagonists are pale shadows of his former characters, representing the twenty-first-century's trendy new morality. In *Angel Mage*, for example, promiscuity and gender fluidity are portrayed as normal and healthy. The antagonist is so obsessed with her love interest she commits mass murder (in fact, she destroys a whole country), but Nix justifies her behavior because she was "only nineteen." The protagonists of the story end up helping the antagonist achieve her ends, and thereby any sense of justice is bypassed or obscured. The story is so morally ambiguous in its message that a parent, much less a preteen, would have trouble receiving any moral clarity by the end. This is exactly why parents need to pre-read contemporary books before buying or borrowing them for their impressionable children.

Going back to our patron saint of story-telling, Chrysostom did not have an explicit theory on story-telling, but his practical guidance implies a belief in its efficacy much like Lewis's. He gives this wisdom to his spiritual

---

53. Guroian, *Tending the Heart*, 24.
54. Lewis, *Abolition of Man*, 24.

children on story-telling: the mother and father should repeatedly tell biblical stories, such as that of Cain and Abel, Jacob's life, or Jesus' resurrection, and eventually have the child tell the story to his parents: "When he has heard it often, ask him too, saying: 'Tell me the story,' so that he may be eager to imitate you. And when he has memorized it thou wilt also tell him how it profits him. The soul indeed, as it receives the story within itself before thou hast elaborated it, is aware that it will benefit."[55]

The telling and retelling of the right story, until the child knows it by heart, is urged by Chrysostom. "With these stories and ten thousand others fortify his hearing," he tells parents, "as thou dost offer him also examples drawn from home."[56] Lewis also saw the return to a good story as a mark of the literate person, who reads and rereads the transformative novel, returning to the book as though visiting an old and cherished friend. "Those who read great works . . . will read the same work ten, twenty or thirty times during the course of their life."[57] The love of the story becomes a thirst, and since the kind of stories of which Lewis and Chrysostom speak are those that expand the moral-spiritual universe and reveal truth, we can speak of thirst in the sense of the Beatitudes: "Blessed *are* they which do hunger and thirst after righteousness: for they shall be filled" (Matt 5:6 KJV).

The stories and imitation of parents shape the child, and Chrysostom warns to keep the child away from gossipers or those who speak "lewdly," as the wrong stories can harm the impressionable child. This advice can be applied to any popular fiction of a gratuitous bent. He also urges age appropriateness, asking that parents wait to tell "fearful tales" until ages eight or ten and to not speak of hell to the child until he is a teenager.[58] Stories can also be adapted by the parents to match the child's maturity and intelligence, as he says, "As the inward sense transcends the child's intelligence, it can be simplified to his level of understanding and implanted in this tender childish intelligence, if we adapt the tale."[59] The next section begins with a case study on a biblical virtue and finishes with a Chrysostom-style guided reading of a Christian novel.

---

55. Chrysostom, "Address on Vainglory," 104.
56. Chrysostom, "Address on Vainglory," 109.
57. Lewis, *Experiment in Criticism*, 25.
58. Chrysostom, "Address on Vainglory," 109.
59. Chrysostom, "Address on Vainglory," 107.

OBEDIENCE AS A HINGE VIRTUE FOR CHILDREN

The desert fathers considered obedience to be the initiatory virtue. I intentionally give a case study of this virtue because obedience in the modern era is regarded with suspicion, if not disdain. The virtue implies an authority, and this is an age that wishes to level all hierarchies, not merely in the name of equality, but because authority itself is an obstacle to radical autonomy. If natural Adam has no bonds tying him to wife or children, father, or mother, then he can have no authority above him. So, obedience becomes a byword to those who see it as nothing more than slavish, blind submission. Yet is this truly what obedience is? Mindless and blind? A slave's virtue? The desert fathers reply to this accusation:

> It is well known that obedience is the chief among the initiatory virtues, for first it displaces presumption and then it engenders humility within us. Thus it becomes, for those who willingly embrace it, a door leading to the love of God. It was because he rejected humility that Adam fell into the lowest depths of Hades. It was because He loved humility that the Lord, in accordance with the divine purpose was obedient to His Father even to the cross and death, although He was in no way inferior to the Father; and so through His own obedience He has freed mankind from the crime of disobedience and leads back to the blessedness of eternal life all who live in obedience. Thus humility should be the first concern of those who are fighting the presumption of the devil, for as we advance it will be a sure guide to all the paths of virtue.[60]

Obedience is a door, or a pathway, to other virtues because it "sets the context" for the spiritual warfare and *askesis* that the disciple undertakes in the journey of spiritual growth.[61] Christlikeness means conforming the will to Christ, and this requires obedience, as the state of the self before this transformation, the "old Adam," is in a state of separation from God. "Just as the result of disobedience is sin so the result of obedience is virtue. And just as disobedience leads to breaking the commandments and to separation from Him who gave them, so obedience leads to keeping the commandments and to union with Him who gave them."[62]

Disobedience turns the self and its will into an idol, an idol that enslaves. Unlike the passivity of the passions, obedience is active. It is a relationship

---

60. G. Palmer et al., *Philokalia*, 1:265.
61. Steenberg, *Beginnings of a Life*, 48.
62. G. Palmer et al., *Philokalia*, 139.

where one is voluntarily abandoning her own self-will and interests to join the will and interests of another person, in this case, God the Father. Thus, obedience to God is the true path of freedom: freedom from the bondage of the passions, from the tyrannical and idolized self-will, and freedom toward one's true end, union with God. Saint Gregory the Great explains aptly, "By the other virtues, we offer God what we possess; but by obedience, we offer our selves to Him. They who obey are conquerors, because by submitting themselves to obedience they triumph over the angels, who fell through disobedience."[63] When Jesus holds up the coin and asks whose image it bears, he is not making a statement about paying taxes (Mark 12:13–17; Matt 22:15–22; Luke 20:19–26). He is telling us, his disciples, that we who were created in the image and likeness of God are to offer our entire selves to him. Following the Master begins with obedience, submitting ourselves in acknowledgment of our nature as image-bearers.

By recognizing what obedience is, as well as its significance concerning spiritual growth, it is incumbent on the parents to instill obedience in their young early on. The tendency of Western culture is to emphasize egalitarianism, which flattens any sense of authority, but this is unbiblical and runs counter to the spirit of Christian freedom. If the child cannot learn to respect and obey the authority of his earthly caretakers, how then can he acknowledge a higher authority? The child obeys her mother and father out of love born through the bond of the parent-child relationship. Likewise, the follower of Christ obeys the will of God out of his love born through the bond of adoption, which forms the living relationship between him and his heavenly Father (Rom 8:23; Rom 9:4; Eph 1:5; Gal 4:5).

As obedience is noteworthy as an initiatory virtue, an example of a child's story is provided below in which obedience is the centerpiece. This reading is offered as both a case study and a practical guide. Chrysostom provided examples of Bible stories that parents could tell their children and instruction on how to teach through these stories. The section below follows his lead with the book *The Silver Chair*. This book belongs to the treasury of Christian stories gifted to us by talented story-tellers. C. S. Lewis's writings may cultivate in his young readers an understanding of Christian concepts and virtues—no less so with *The Silver Chair*, the sixth book of his *Chronicles of Narnia* series. The following reveals what biblical truth parents can glean from a Christian novel and ways they can discuss the story with their child.

---

63. Gregory the Great, as quoted in Steenberg, *Beginnings of a Life*, 50.

A GUIDED READING OF THE SILVER CHAIR

The Silver Chair is an adventure story featuring three characters on a quest to find the lost crown prince of Narnia. There are certain key points in the story that parents can highlight after reading the story aloud. This conversation between parent and child is not a test, an interrogation, or a lesson but the kind of lively discussion one would expect in a book club. The parent and the child are both enthusiasts of the story. The parents might let the children "go first," sharing their favorite parts of the story. After the children have their turns, the following highlighted passages, with the embedded biblical truth, might be introduced by the parents as they take their turn. Since the book is long, it would be read aloud daily, chapter by chapter, until complete.

Chapters 1 through 2

The story begins with a schoolgirl, Jill Pole, hiding in the school yard from bullies. The school she attends is an "experimental" school that allows the students free rein. The result of this lack of structure is rather like a *Lord of the Flies* scenario, where the largest and strongest students tyrannize the rest of the student body. There is no real discipline by the administration, which makes the school a nightmare to attend for most of the students. Jill is crying behind some shrubbery, having recently escaped her tormentors, and is found by a schoolmate, Eustace Scrubb.[64] Eustace and Jill are the same age and are classmates, and Eustace sympathizes with Jill because he has also had encounters with the bullies.

Eustace is different in one way, however. During the holidays, he was swept into Narnia with two cousins and travelled by sea through the magical land. The previous adventure left its mark on Eustace, and he tells Jill that if they call on Somebody called Aslan, they might be able to escape the school and their tormentors. Jill is not sure if Eustace is telling the truth about a magical world, but she is desperate enough to give it a try. Just as the children repeat Aslan's name three times, they hear the bullies coming for them, and they try to escape by way of a door to the moors, a door which is always locked. This time, however, the door inexplicably opens. Instead of the bleak moors, the children see sunshine and trees, brilliant flora and jewel-colored birds. The children jump through the door to the other place.

The awestruck students walk through the towering forest, only to find a steep drop-off. The precipice is so high that even the clouds seem small

---

64. Eustace was introduced in Lewis's *Voyage of the Dawn Treader*.

as they hover far below. Jill, seeing that Eustace is afraid of heights, mean-spiritedly teases him by stepping to the very edge. This backfires on her, however, and she almost falls. She is saved by Eustace, who grabs her and shoves her away from the cliff but, in so doing, goes over the edge. Suddenly, an enormous animal is beside Jill. It is a lion, and he is blowing gusts of wind from his mouth, making Eustace fly away from them at a great speed. The lion then walks away, leaving Jill alone. She cries in shame for what she did, then gets up. She is thirsty and begins to look for something to drink.

She follows the sound of running water until she finds a stream, but the lion sits by, and so she is afraid to go near the water. The lion tells her, "If you're thirsty, you may drink."[65] Jill is so scared of the beast that she tries to negotiate with him, but he makes no promises that he will not eat her. Finally, despite her fear, she forces herself to drink. "It was the worst thing she ever had to do, but she went forward to the stream, knelt down, and began scooping up water in her hand. It was the coldest, most refreshing water she had ever tasted."[66]

Once she has quenched her thirst, the lion questions her, asking her where the boy is. Jill is forced to admit, through a series of questions, that Eustace fell because she was "showing off."[67] The lion is pleased with her honesty and tells her to "do so no more." He then explains that she and Eustace were called into this magical world for a purpose and that this purpose has now become more difficult by what she has done. Jill is unsure of this. She tells the lion that no one called her and Eustace; they instead were calling on Somebody. The lion contradicts her, saying, "You would not have called to me unless I had been calling you."

"Then you are Somebody, sir?" said Jill.

"I am. And now hear your task."[68]

With the confirmation that the lion is the Somebody, Aslan, on whom Eustace and Jill had called, the reader/listener is led to several conclusions. One, admitting wrongdoing is the right thing to do and invites forgiveness and mercy. More specifically, repentance is called for. This means admitting the wrong, learning from the consequences, and not repeating the same mistake. Repentance is required by God if we want a relationship with him. The second conclusion is that when we call upon our Maker, he has always called us first. Prayer is a response to God's invitation to relationship. Third, when we ask for deliverance in times of need, God answers. Fourth, when

---

65. Lewis, *Silver Chair*, 21.
66. Lewis, *Silver Chair*, 23.
67. Lewis, *Silver Chair*, 24.
68. Lewis, *Silver Chair*, 25.

we are thirsty and in need, God is the ultimate source, the living water that satisfies completely. Finally, fear truly is the beginning of wisdom, for in fear we approach the Creator. Jill is terrified of the lion, but she steps forward and drinks when he beckons.

The lion explains to Jill that the king of Narnia is dying, and his only child and heir has disappeared. Jill receives the order from Aslan to seek the lost prince. "I lay on you this command, that you seek this lost prince until you have either found him and brought him to his father's house, or else died in the attempt, or else gone back to your own world."[69] Aslan proceeds to describe four signs that the girl must remember in order to find the lost Prince Rilian. Aslan repeatedly emphasizes the importance of these signs and makes Jill memorize them before he sends her off: "'Say them to yourself when you wake in the morning and when you lie down at night, and when you wake up in the middle of the night. And whatever strange things may happen to you, let nothing turn your mind from the signs.... Remember the signs and believe the signs. Nothing else matters.'"[70]

Aslan's instructions recall the greatest commandment given to the Israelites in the wilderness, the following command in Deuteronomy 6:6-7: "And these words that I command you today shall be on your heart. You shall teach them diligently to your children, and shall talk of them when you sit in your house, and when you walk by the way, and when you lie down, and when you rise." Obedience is required to complete the task. The story concerns many virtues, but they all hinge on one virtue, *obedience*. In *The Silver Chair*, this means obedience to the Creator and Lawgiver of Narnia, Aslan. There is a reason Lewis describes this first meeting with Aslan as on a mountaintop. Aslan tells Jill, "Here on the mountain I have spoken clearly: I will not often do so down in Narnia."[71] Like Moses in his first encounter with God, Jill is terrified but approaches anyway. Again like Moses, Jill questions who the lion is and is told "I am." As on Mount Sinai, the result of speaking face to face with God is that of humility and obedience. In humility, Jill admits to herself that it is her fault that the responsibility of remembering the signs is not shared with Eustace, and in obedience, she accepts this responsibility. "Jill remembered very well that if there was no time to spare, that was her own fault. 'If I hadn't made such a fool of myself, Scrubb and I would have been going together. And he'd have heard all the instructions as well as me,' she thought. So she did as she was told."[72]

69. Lewis, *Silver Chair*, 25.
70. Lewis, *Silver Chair*, 27.
71. Lewis, *Silver Chair*, 27.
72. Lewis, *Silver Chair*, 26.

Chapters 3 through 9

After receiving her task from the lion, Jill is blown off the mountain on the lion's breath to the coast of Narnia, where she finds Eustace. She tells him the first sign to look for, as it depends on his previous experience in Narnia, but confusion and lost time make them miss their chance. This means that instead of having the king's help, they must make do with whatever they can get. Aid comes by way of the parliament of owls, who fly them to the marshlands to a Marsh-wiggle named Puddleglum. Puddleglum, unlike the other Marsh-wiggles, is adventurous. He agrees to help the children by acting as a guide into the northern country of Ettinsmoor. Ettinsmoor is dangerous and full of giants, but Aslan's signs to Jill indicate that the prince is lost somewhere in the ruined city of the giants. With their guide, the children head into the wild wastelands of the north.

Jill is diligent in repeating the signs as she was told. She shares them with her companions, Eustace and Puddleglum, and they set off seeking the second sign. The adventurers come to a bridge and meet a strange pair of travelers. One is a beautiful lady attired in green astride a white horse. Her companion is a knight in black armor whose face is entirely shrouded by his visor. The lady speaks to the children, and they trustingly tell her of their search for the ruined city. Upon hearing this, the lady tells them that they will find warm beds, good food, and gentle giants at Harfang, and that they should mention "she of the Green Kirtle."[73] After the knight and lady depart, all the children can think about is the comfortable lodgings and kind hosts that they will find in Harfang. Puddleglum tries to warn them about trusting strangers, but neither Jill nor Eustace believe such a beautiful lady could be lying to them.

After this event, things worsen. First, the terrain becomes even more inhospitable and frigid. Secondly, the lady's words haunt the children, until all they can think about is reaching Harfang and enjoying a full meal and good sleep. This completely wipes any thoughts of their actual task from their mind, and "they never talked about Aslan, or even about the prince now. And Jill gave up her habit of repeating the signs over to herself every night and morning."[74] Through road fatigue and complacency, Jill forgets the signs and grows angry when Puddleglum asks her about them.

When they reach Harfang, they are welcomed, fed, clothed, and given luxurious rooms, just as the lady promised. However, Jill and Eustace realize too late that they are virtually prisoners in the castle. They cannot leave

---

73. Lewis, *Silver Chair*, 89.
74. Lewis, *Silver Chair*, 93.

to continue their quest or find the third sign, which Jill cannot remember, although she tries. This striving toward obedience is met with grace, as Aslan helps Jill in a dream to remember the third sign. Once Jill realizes that they must go under a ruined city, she and her fellow adventurers struggle to figure out how they can escape the castle. Finding a way out becomes imperative as they learn that they are going to be eaten by the king and queen during the Autumn Feast of the giants.

Parents reading up to this point with their child have many insights they can discuss. As in real life, things go more smoothly when living according to God's will. Yet even when we are obedient, life is still filled with challenges and dangerous trials that can cause the Christian to stumble and fall. The recourse is always to seek help from God and our brothers and sisters in Christ.

Jill and her companions were doing better, despite the hardships of travelling by foot through wilderness, when Jill kept Aslan's words in mind and remembered his signs. When she trusted the smooth words of an attractive stranger, however, she and Eustace were tempted by the promise of creature comforts. Their focus turned from Aslan's goal to another, lesser goal. This caused them to end up in a more difficult situation than needed, putting the success of their quest in doubt, and they almost lost their lives to the giants' bellies. Material wealth is a gift from God, but the Christian is not to seek it as her aim in life. God provides all earthly needs, sustaining all people, whether good or bad. Those who truly seek him, though, must sometimes sacrifice earthly wants if they become obstacles to God himself. Reminding our children of the apostle John's paraphrase of the two greatest commands is helpful and can easily be remembered: "And he has given us this command: Anyone who loves God must also love their brother and sister" (1 John 4:21 NIV). Additionally, this verse can be paired with Matthew 6:33, "But seek first his kingdom and his righteousness, and all these things will be given to you as well." God commands that his children seek a relationship with him first, before any other thing or person in life. Secondly, he commands that we live according to his will, and finally, he promises that the necessities of life will be provided along the way.

Jill and Eustace stop listening to the good advice of their older and wiser companion, Puddleglum, who never fails to direct them to keep their minds and hearts on Aslan's quest. Puddleglum repeatedly advises them *not* to listen to the green lady, *not* to go to Harfang Castle, and to remember the signs given by Aslan. Yet the children ignore him. Still, Puddleglum never abandons them to the dangers they face, even though the children put his life in equal danger, and he remains loyal to Aslan and the goal. Puddleglum is not as attractive in looks or speech as the lady, yet he proved a true guide and friend. Parents can use his example to remind their children not to trust the flattering words of a stranger, not to fall in with bad companions because of their fashionable style or way of talking, and to listen to true friends who remain alongside them even in bad times.

Chapters 10 through 16

The three companions barely escape Harfang with their lives. After Aslan helps Jill to remember the third sign in a dream, they figure out a plan to reach their destination, a world underneath the ruined city of the giants. Upon entering the undercity, they are immediately captured by Earthmen and forced to journey through sunless tunnels. The cavernous world they encounter is terrible, riddled with creatures and people who have lost their way and fallen into an enchanted sleep. None of this is reassuring, but the adventurers do not lose hope, even as the Earthmen take them by force to the underground city of their queen. The adventurers still have one more sign to guide them.

They are taken to the queen's castle and her knight. Here they find that he was the black knight they encountered above, and the lady in green is the queen of the underworld. The young knight tells them a strange tale, that he is to be king of the overworld once the queen has finished tunneling into Narnia, and that she will be his wife. He also explains that she saved him from a mysterious curse that ails him. Puddleglum warns the children about taking the story for granted: "There's a stronger smell of danger and lies and magic and treason about this land than I've ever smelled before."[75]

The knight tells them that they will see his curse firsthand, as he is soon to be tied to a chair. He makes them promise not to cut him loose, as he becomes insane during this time and nothing he says can be trusted. The children agree to hide in another room while his handlers bind him. When they hear him moaning, the three return to the room.

Obedience is the hardest part of the quest, even as the last sign is found. Fearing bodily harm or worse, the companions must free the bound knight from a silver chair, because he invokes the name of Aslan as he cries for help. "I adjure you to set me free. By all fears and all loves, by the bright skies of Overland, by the great Lion, by Aslan himself, I charge you."[76] This was the last sign, that the one they meet who calls the name of Aslan is the lost prince. The children and Puddleglum release him, and Prince Rilian immediately picks up his sword and destroys the chair. They now know that

75. Lewis, *Silver Chair*, 161.
76. Lewis, *Silver Chair*, 166.

the queen of Underland is a witch who wishes to rule Narnia through an enchanted puppet-king whom she kidnapped many years before.

The queen herself enters the room and sees what has happened. She uses her magical powers, attempting to fog the minds of the prince and his helpers, and nearly succeeds in making them forget their own world and Aslan himself. Yet Puddleglum, the most obedient servant of Aslan, dispels the enchantment pressing upon them by reminding them, "I'm on Aslan's side even if there isn't any Aslan to lead it. I'm going to live as like a Narnian as I can even if there isn't any Narnia."[77] When the witch loses her hold on their minds, she transforms into a giant green serpent and tries to squeeze Rilian to death. With the help of Eustace and Puddleglum, Rilian beheads the serpent, the same beast, it turns out, who murdered his mother. Justice is finally served, and it happened only through obedience.

Happily, the inhabitants of Underland are freed from the witch's enchantment, and all return to their homes deeper into the earth. Prince Rilian and the children escape to the surface, and Rilian reunites with his father, obtaining his blessing before the father, the old King Caspian, dies. The children are returned to the mountain of Aslan, where they see a young King Caspian, who now lives in Aslan's country in the land beyond the sea. The door opens, and the children return to the schoolyard to face the bullies but, this time, with Aslan and Caspian at their back. After the defeat of the bullies, Aslan and Caspian return to Aslan's country, and Jill and Eustace are left to a school that undergoes a profound change for the better.

These last chapters are deeply eschatological. This book might offer children their first inkling of what awaits them if they follow the way of Christ to the end. Prince Rilian's bondage by the serpent-queen and his subsequent half-life in the Underworld are an image of death and satanic bondage. Yet as Rilian calls out to Aslan, as he must have for years beneath the earth, Aslan responds, delivering him from enslavement through the hands of obedient children. The prince's destruction of the silver chair is the literal destruction of the chains of his enslavement to sin and evil. His emergence out of the deep is akin to the waters of baptism, but on another level, it is a reimaging of Jesus Christ's emergence from the tomb. "Pale though he was from long imprisonment in the Deep Lands, dressed in black, dusty, disheveled, and weary, there was something in his face and air no one could mistake. That look is in the face of all true Kings of Narnia, who rule by the will of Aslan . . . . Instantly every head was bared and every knee was bent."[78]

---

77. Lewis, *Silver Chair*, 182.
78. Lewis, *Silver Chair*, 225.

The effect of being in the presence of the true King marks the face of those who spend time in his presence, as Jill notes of Eustace, who has spent more time in Narnia, spoken more with Aslan, fought alongside kings, and has thus grown from a petulant, horrid child into something else: "She saw that his face was quite changed. He looked much more like the Prince than like the old Scrubb at Experiment House. For all his adventures, and the days when he had sailed with King Caspian, were coming back to him."[79] As Moses's face shines from being in the presence of God, the follower of Christ is transformed the longer one abides in Christ.

When the children return to the mountain for one last meeting with Aslan before they are sent back to England, they see how young King Caspian is again, "because of people having no particular age in Aslan's country."[80] Death and age have no place in God's kingdom either. When the children hope to stay with Aslan and Caspian, Aslan tells them, "When you meet me here again, you will have come to stay. But not now. You must go back to your own world for a little while."[81] Just as we are called together to form the body of Christ, we are also called into the world, for just a little while, that the world might be saved through us. God's promise is echoed to us through a children's story, and in the reading of this story together, heaven enters the child's imagination.

SUMMARY

Chrysostom saw story-telling as a tool of great power in molding the morality and spirituality of the child, in that the right kinds of stories inculcated biblical truth within the young. Contemporary thinkers like Alasdair MacIntyre echo the importance of the story as part of what keeps a tradition alive. Christians are part of a living tradition, an adventure of faith lived out in a community of travelers with the same destination: the kingdom of God. Throughout its history, the Christian tradition returns again and again to its core story, as related in the four Gospels and Scripture.

In the modern era, the story, in the sense of Chrysostom's view as a truth-bearer, appears most vividly in the novel. At its heart, the novel is meant to guide the listener or reader onto the road of repentance and conversion, just as the novelist is also travelling on that road. The hero or heroine of the novel is an external mediator of the desire for God and also a

---

79. Lewis, *Silver Chair*, 206.
80. Lewis, *Silver Chair*, 239.
81. Lewis, *Silver Chair*, 240.

created agent for the vicarious practice of Christian virtue, as the soul seeks transformation into Christlikeness.

Other contemporary thinkers—Karen Swallow Prior, Joseph Bottum, Vigen Guroian, and C. S. Lewis—showed us how novels teach children how to think. Their work on the novel extends and deepens Chrysostom's thought on the nature of story-telling. Real literacy, or the ability to read well—deeply, attentively, and critically—cultivates not only virtue but the conscience through empathy and vicarious experience. The conscience is the hub of the wheel of moral expression, and it only becomes sensitive through cultivation. This cultivation of the heart protects the reader from indoctrination. "By starving the sensibility of our pupils we only make them easier prey to the propagandist when he comes. For famished nature will be avenged and a hard heart is no infallible protection against a soft head."[82] Instead of indoctrination, reading the classical novel initiates the reader into the tradition. On education, Lewis notes, "The old kind was a kind of propagation—men transmitting manhood to men; the new is merely propaganda." The premodern education proffered by Chrysostom is the propagation—the golden cord—and story-telling one of the golden threads.

Reading stories as a family may be the easiest of Chrysostom's three elements in tackling moral formation. The spiritual exercises, such as prayer, require habitual practice. One prays throughout the hours of the day, in the morning and evening at the very least, but also before (and possibly after) mealtimes, and at the onset and completion of any task. This is harder, requiring mindfulness, discipline, and the parent actively mentoring/modeling the practice for the child. Positive *mimesis* springs naturally from such mentorship. This second element, imitation, is perhaps the hardest element of the pedagogy, as it requires even more attention and relies on self-discipline learned through *askesis* on the part of the mentor. Yet story-time requires no such struggle. It is easy to fit into the day, either before naps or bedtime, and as the third supporting pillar in Chrysostom's framework, story-telling will give the family a place to begin shaping character and give the parents needed confidence that they *can* be the moral leader their children need them to be. Prayer, and eventually other spiritual exercises, can be practiced in conjunction with story-telling, as well as modeling the right conduct and behavior. The next and last chapter will review how Chrysostom's three pillars work together and conclude this discussion on his moral and spiritual education for the Christian family.

---

82. Lewis, *Abolition of Man*, 14.

Conclusion

The Golden Cord

Now that we are coming to the end of this journey together, what ground have we covered, and where are we going? We began with Alasdair MacIntyre's famous description of a post-apocalyptic world in order to situate us within our twenty-first century moral setting. MacIntyre believes the moral dystopia of Western civilization results from the stripping away of moral meaning from its original contexts. His remedy is to return to some form of tradition to revive objective moral standards. I accepted this challenge by arguing for a premodern moral education and presented Chrysostom as a teacher and guide for the Christian family. By analyzing and describing the elements of Chrysostom's Christian education presented in "On Vainglory," the preceding five chapters retrieved and expanded upon his thought with the help of contemporary thinkers in a historical recapturing of his moral framework. The three main elements of Chrysostom's moral and spiritual education prescribed for families were spiritual exercise, imitation, and story-telling. These elements, when grounded by premodern Christianity's theanthropic ethic, build on and support each other and function holistically.

In chapter 1, we went through how MacIntyre's tradition as morality stance is one of many alternatives from which to choose. The main difference between his moral view of tradition as the context for morality and these alternatives is that it derives from a pre-Enlightenment perspective on what moral meaning is, while the competitors for morality were born from the Enlightenment. Six alternatives for morality were considered and analyzed. These included emotivism, subjectivism, Nietzschean existentialism, liberal theology, psychology, and gnosticism. These alternative views of morality, which alternately conflict and complement each other, created the morally ambiguous landscape that MacIntyre describes. Thus, MacIntyre concludes that emotivism is the unintentional moral position taken by the West.

In order to offer a premodern alternative to post-Enlightenment moralities, St. John Chrysostom was our guide in working toward a tradition-based system of moral education. Chrysostom lived during a time that was in many ways parallel to the Western modern era. He spent his life in two cosmopolitan cities, both known for their wealth and status in the known world—a trading hub, Antioch, and the Eastern imperial capital, Constantinople. The citizens of these cities had struggles and concerns similar to those of contemporary twenty-first-century Westerners. The Christians of Chrysostom's church had to navigate and learn how to be a Christian in a prosperous pluralistic society with all of its entertainments and temptations. The question of how to raise children as Christians was one of the key concerns Chrysostom attempted to address in homilies and his treatise "On Vainglory." His preaching on the subject of moral and spiritual formation is highly practical and pastoral, which makes him sympathetic to the thesis. The breadth of his work is vast, with over eight hundred extant documents, giving this project ample material from which to draw.

I drew from the surviving corpus of Chrysostom's work but also explored the work of other patristic sources of the first Christian millennium. By relying on these ancient primary sources, this study of a tradition-based morality hopes to transcend the various Christian traditions that have developed over the centuries. By building on the premodern, theanthropic ethic, I also led us through an earlier Christian understanding of theology and ethics. This guide hopefully succeeded in stripping away some preconceptions and ethical assumptions by relying on an older, lesser known tradition of Christianity. In using this method, a corrective was provided for post-Enlightenment theology that is built upon many of the concepts discussed in the review of alternative moralities.

Another recurring theme of the journey was to walk beside contemporary thinkers to enrich our understanding of Chrysostom's project, specifically the guides René Girard and Alasdair MacIntyre. The infusion of an ancient pedagogy into Christian moral education with contemporary concepts was meant to push the boundaries of how we think of Christian discipleship, moral/spiritual formation, and the *telos* of family life. In many ways, this book is meant to challenge Christian families to a deeper spirituality, just as Chrysostom tried to push his congregations beyond the cake-frosting Christianity so popular in his culture and ours.

As explained above, the first chapter began the discussion into moral formation of the family by first framing it within the context of competing moral views. I did this to focus our attention and offer a better alternative in the form of a tradition-based, theanthropic ethic. The first competing viewpoints presented were emotivism and subjectivism as implicit forms of morality practiced in current culture. Emotivists view morality as nothing more than opinions and feelings, while subjectivists believe in some form of moral relativity. The next alternative offered for examination and critique was within the area of moral philosophy. Nietzschean existentialism, with its emphases on authenticity and the freedom of choice, was discussed as an influential moral concept. Liberal theology was the fourth alternative morality. This way of interpreting reality and morality views religion and morality as dependent upon the single individual's self-consciousness and emotions. The therapeutic movement was the fifth alternative. The review of this area of moral thinking examined how psychology has triumphed over religion for many people in the modern era, with self-actualization becoming the only human *telos*. Finally, modern gnosticism was discussed as a sixth alternative to morality, as a religious phenomenon that, when mingled with the political thought of nation-states, manifests in a plethora of forms.

These six alternative moral perspectives gave a richer understanding of the modern moral dystopia pictured in MacIntyre's hypothesis. By studying the undercurrent of moral thought in contemporary culture, we saw how these alternative streams of morality prevail in the attitudes of individuals, even Christians. This is the atmosphere in which Christians must raise their children, and we now understand MacIntyre's urgency a little better, in his call to go back to an earlier moral vision of education.

All of these six post-Enlightenment streams of thought are fundamentally anti-Christian, and they all attack the biblical understanding of humanhood. Human will, emotions, and autonomy are presented as the chief ends of humankind, with the purposeful denial and rejection of God as Creator and humanity as creation in his image. The crisis of the current age demands a response from Christians, which is the main reason this thesis defends a moral education of children and families. It is a return to the morality of tradition, which Chrysostom pictures as a chain linking the generations of master to disciple, elder to youth, parent to child.

The chapters that followed provided background and support for Chrysostom's plan for the family. Chapter 2 framed Chrysostom within his historical and theological position. It set the stage for a better understanding of his moral and spiritual education for the family. His educational edifice was to be built on three supporting pillars: (1) *askesis* practiced by the entire family, (2) the child's emulation of spiritual mentors within the church, and (3) the parents' use of story-telling as a tool for the cultivation of the child's inner moral world.

Chapters 3 and 4 had a twofold goal: present two of Chrysostom's pillars and at the same time situate them within his premodern theology-ethic. Chapter 3 focused on *askesis* and how it relates the human relationship with God in Trinity, in terms of the incarnation, grace, and, most of all, spiritual formation. The main sources and voices besides Chrysostom's were Vladimir Lossky and the desert fathers found through *The Philokalia*.

Chapter 4 examined Chrysostom's second building block in detail, that of emulation. Emulation was contextualized within his theological anthropology and his understanding of doctrines of sin, death, evil. A premodern description of the human moral capacities as part of the image-bearing nature was given. Next, a discussion of the fall's effect on these moral capacities was examined. Emulation was then analyzed as a human capacity for learning and discussed in terms of mimetic theory. Finally, a discussion of positive *mimesis* was approached through Chrysostom's belief in modeling as a method for moral formation in children.

Chapter 5, the last leg of our journey, took us through story-telling. The chapter began with a discussion of how Chrysostom defined and used stories. Chrysostom had a broad understanding of what constituted a story, seeing it as basically any communication presented in narrative form, which included drama, Bible narratives, pagan epic poetry, fables, and gossip. He saw stories as a vehicle for either virtue or vice and considered a story worthy of being told to a child only if it contained biblical truth.

After this discussion, we moved through Alasdair MacIntyre's concept of tradition and the significance of story-telling within tradition. For MacIntyre, virtues exist within communities of tradition. Stories are used to cultivate and maintain each community's virtues, transferring wisdom from one generation to the next. Chrysostom echoes this concept with his metaphor of the golden chain, or cord.

The chapter then stretched his thoughts on story-telling to story's modern form, which developed most distinctly as the novel. In this conversation, the vicarious nature of story-telling was examined through the work of Karen Swallow Prior, Joseph Bottum, Vigen Guroian, and René Girard. These thinkers helped to delineate what made the story so important as a conveyer of biblical truth and Christian virtue. Finally, we traveled through a guided tour of a Christian classic, C. S. Lewis's *The Silver Chair*. This guide shows how parents can teach their children about the Christian virtue of obedience through a story.

Looking back, we travelled together through time and space, spanned centuries and movements in Christian thought, all to pursue the question of what God's *telos* is for the Christian family.

LIFE IN THE WASTELAND

We stop our tour together here, but we both know that we have a long road to travel ahead, as our pursuit of the godly family is just beginning. Indeed, it is one small part in our overall Christian life, as we attempt to obediently walk in Christ's footsteps, the way of righteousness. The intent of this book was to provide for the family an alternative vision of moral education, one rooted in ancient Christianity and its theology-ethic, and to resist the anti-Christian moral dystopia of current culture. I believe that St. John Chrysostom's moral vision for the family is still a valid option, as the preceding chapters have shown. His blueprint for the "little church" is meant to transform families into communities of little Christs. He says as much to parents in his "Homily 21 on Ephesians," "Never say, this is the business of monks. Am I making a monk of him [the child]? No. There is no need he should become a monk.... Make him a Christian. For it is of all things necessary for laymen to be acquainted with the lessons derived from this source; but especially for children."[1]

Whether it is teaching obedience through *The Silver Chair*, eternity through *The Little Mermaid*, or true friendship through *The Wind in the Willows*, the stories told embed themselves in the inner mind of the child. What we are exposed to, especially early on, is more influential than weekly sermons from a pulpit. The little church can follow Chrysostom's pattern for the Christian life of the family. Simply going to church is not enough for moral and spiritual growth. Yes, life must adapt to the rhythm and flow of church life but also to the discipline of *spiritual exercise*, the intentional *imitation* of mature Christians, and the exposure to the spiritual richness of the great *stories* of the faith.

Perhaps the best way to end is to recall the Exodus. In many ways, the Exodus is the key story in the Judeo-Christian tradition. For the Christian, Moses is a prefiguration of Jesus Christ, the good shepherd who obeys the will of God and delivers his flock from the enemy. Moral development begins in infancy, with caregivers the first models and teachers. If the Exodus is taken as a metaphor for life, then life for the Christian is the wilderness, the training ground where the Israelite prepares for entrance into the promised land. The wilderness is also a wasteland, and we live in a moral wasteland.

In terms of Chrysostom's system of education, his golden cord, *askesis* is the way the former slaves, freed from Egyptian captivity, learn to live and think like freemen and freewomen. Being reborn in Christ at baptism is only the beginning of deliverance through the Red Sea. The former sinner

---

1. Chrysostom, "Homily 21," in *Homilies on Ephesians*, 154.

is still in bondage to old ways of thinking, to old habits and addictions that enslave. By journeying through the wilderness, the people of God must change, transforming into citizens of the new country. The Israelites might be free, but they still yearn for Egypt. A change must occur. Yet God grants his struggling children guides along the way, spiritual mentors like Moses and Miriam, Joshua and Caleb. As a community of newly freed slaves, God gives the stories and the laws, the treasury of wisdom that teaches his ways. Even if we should die in the wilderness, we see a glimmer of his kingdom, the kingdom beyond the Jordan. We know that one day, when we finally arrive, we will abide with him forever.

This is where I leave us. I hope St. John Chrysostom's golden cord will be grasped as the lifeline that it is. Chrysostom gifted his generation of Christians with a vision of beatitude for their whole family. This vision is worth a second glance for Christian families of this generation, too.

Bibliography

Alison, James. *The Joy of Being Wrong: Original Sin through Easter Eyes.* New York: Crossroad, 1998.
Antonello, Pierpaolo, and Heather Webb, eds. *Mimesis, Desire, and the Novel: René Girard and Literary Criticism.* East Lansing: Michigan State University Press, 2015.
Athanasius. *The Incarnation of the Word of God.* Translated by a religious of CSMVS Th. London: Centenary, 1944.
Augustine. "What the Cause of the Blessedness of the Good Angels Is, and What the Cause of the Misery of the Wicked." Bible Hub. https://biblehub.com/library/augustine/city_of_god/chapter_6_what_the_cause_of.htm.
Bashaw, Jennifer Garcia. "Jesus, Girard, and Dystopian Literature." *Perspectives in Religious Studies* 43, no. 1 (Spring 2016) 73–86.
Bellinger, Charles K. *The Genealogy of Violence: Reflections on Creation, Freedom, and Evil.* Oxford, UK: Oxford University Press, 2001.
———. *The Trinitarian Self: The Key to the Puzzle of Violence.* Eugene, OR: Pickwick, 2008.
Bottum, Joseph. *The Decline of the Novel.* South Bend, IN: St. Augustine's, 2019.
Buber, Martin. *Between Man and Man.* New York: Macmillian, 1978.
Budziszewski, J. *Commentary on Thomas Aquinas's Treatise on Law.* New York: Cambridge University Press, 2014.
Bunge, Gabriel. *Dragon's Wine and Angel's Bread: The Teaching of Evagrius Ponticus on Anger and Meekness.* Crestwood, NY: St Vladimir's Seminary Press, 2009.
Carroll, Lewis. *Alice's Adventures in Wonderland and Other Stories.* New York: Barnes and Noble, 2010.
Chrysostom, John. "An Address on Vainglory and the Right Way for Parents to Bring Up Their Children." In *Christianity and Pagan Culture in the Later Roman Empire*, translated by M. L. W. Laistner, 85–122. Ithaca, NY: Cornell University, 1951.
———. *Homilies on Galatians, Ephesians, Philippians.* Edited by Philip Schaff. Translated by John Broadus. Nicene and Post-Nicene Fathers, 1st ser., 13. Grand Rapids: Eerdmans, 1889. Kindle.
———. *Homilies on the Gospel of Saint Matthew.* Translated by Philip Schaff. Nicene and Post-Nicene Fathers, 1st ser., 10. Whitefish, MO: Kessinger, 2006. Kindle.
———. *On Marriage and Family Life.* Translated by Catherine P. Roth and David Anderson. Crestwood, NY: St Vladimir's Seminary Press, 1986.
———. *On the Priesthood; Ascetic Treatise; Select Homilies and Letters; Homilies on the Statues.* Edited by Philip Schaff. Nicene and Post-Nicene Fathers, 1st ser., 9. New York: Christian Literature, 1889.

Chrysostom, John. Edited and translated by Anne Marie Malingrey. *Sur la vaine gloire et l'éducation des enfants*. Sources Chrétiennes 188. Paris: Cerf, 1972.

Collodi, Carlo. *Pinocchio*. New York: Sterling, 2016.

Constitutions of the Holy Apostles. Edited by Alexander Roberts and James Donaldson. Ante-Nicene Fathers 7. New York: Charles Scribner's Sons, 1913.

Cyril of Jerusalem. *Cyril of Jerusalem, Gregory Nazianzen*. Edited by Philip Schaff and Henry Wace. Translated by Charles Gordon Browne and James Edward Swallow. Nicene and Post-Nicene Fathers, 2nd ser., 7. Grand Rapids: Eerdmans, 1893.

Delsol, Chantal. *The Unlearned Lessons of the Twentieth Century: An Essay on Late Modernity*. Translated by Robin Dick. Wilmington, DE: ISI, 2006.

Drobner, Hubertus R. *The Fathers of the Church: A Comprehensive Introduction*. Translated by Siegfried S. Schatzmann. Grand Rapids: Baker, 2007.

Durant, William. *Story of Philosophy: The Lives and Opinions of the Greater Philosophers*. New York: Pocket, 1926.

Ephrem. "Lenten Prayer of St. Ephrem." Orthodox Church in America, n.d. https://www.oca.org/orthodoxy/prayers/lenten-prayer-of-st.-ephrem.

Fielding, Henry. *The History of Tom Jones, a Foundling*. Gutenberg, Dec. 29, 2002; last updated Mar. 15, 2018. https://www.gutenberg.org/files/6593/6593-h/6593-h.htm.

Florovsky, Georges. *Bible, Church, Tradition*. Vol. 1 of *An Eastern Orthodox View*. Belmont, MA: Nordland, 1972.

Fletcher, Joseph. *Situation Ethics: The New Morality*. Philadelphia: Westminster, 1966.

Garrels, Scott R. "Human Imitation: Historical, Philosophical, and Scientific Perspectives." In *Mimesis and Science: Empirical Research on Imitation and the Mimetic Theory of Culture and Religion*, edited by Scott R. Garrels, 1–38. East Lansing: Michigan State University Press, 2011.

Geronimi, Clyde, et al., dirs. *Alice in Wonderland*. Burbank, CA: Walt Disney Animation Studios, 1951.

Girard, René. *Battling to the End: Conversations with Benoît Chantre*. East Lansing: Michigan State University Press, 2005.

———. *Deceit, Desire and the Novel: Self and Other in Literary Structure*. Translated by Yvonne Freccero. Baltimore: Johns Hopkins University Press, 1966.

———. *The Girard Reader*. Edited by James G. Williams. New York: Crossroad Herder, 1996.

———. *I See Satan Fall like Lightning*. Translated by James G. Williams. Maryknoll, NY: Orbis, 2001.

———. *Violence and the Sacred*. Translated by Patrick Gregory. Baltimore: Johns Hopkins University Press, 1977.

Girard, René, et al. *Evolution and Conversion*. London: Bloomsbury, 2017.

———. *Things Hidden since the Foundation of the World*. Translated by Stephen Bann and Michael Metteer. Stanford, CA: Stanford University Press, 1987.

Goff, William. *Dynamic Discipleship: The Biblical Force of Christlikeness*. Self-published, 2018.

Gragnolati, Manuele, and Heather Webb. "*Dubbiosi Disiri*." In *Mimesis, Desire, and the Novel*, edited by Pierpaolo Antonello and Heather Webb, 113–31. East Lansing: Michigan State University Press, 2015.

Green, Melody. "Jesus, Girard, and Twentieth-Century Fantasy for Young Adults." *Studies in the Literary Imagination* 46.2, (Fall 2013), 19–33.

Gregory of Nyssa. *The Life of Moses*. Translated by Abraham J. Malherbe and Everett Ferguson. New York: Paulist, 1978.
Guroian, Vigen. "The Ecclesial Family: John Chrysostom on Parenthood and Children." In *The Child in Christian Thought*, edited by Marcia J. Bunge, 61–77. Grand Rapids: Eerdmans, 2001.
———. *Incarnate Love: Essays in Orthodox Ethics*. Notre Dame: IN: Notre Dame University Press, 2002.
———. *Tending the Heart of Virtue: How Classic Stories Awaken a Child's Moral Imagination*. New York: Oxford University Press, 1998.
Harakas, Stanley S. *Health and Medicine in the Eastern Orthodox Tradition: Faith, Liturgy, and Wholeness*. Minneapolis: Light and Life Publishing, 1990.
———. "An Orthodox Christian Approach to the 'New Morality.'" *Greek Orthodox Theological Review* 15, no. 1 (1970) 107–39.
———. *Toward Transfigured Life: The Theoria of Eastern Orthodox Ethics*. Minneapolis: Light and Life, 1983.
Harlow, Mary, and Ray Laurence, eds. *A Cultural History of Childhood and Family in Antiquity*. Oxford, UK: Berg, 2018.
Hauerwas, Stanley. *After Christendom?* Nashville: Abingdon, 1991.
———. *A Community of Character: Toward a Constructive Christian Social Ethic*. Notre Dame, IN: University of Notre Dame Press, 1981.
Haven, Cynthia L. *Evolution of Desire*. East Lansing: Michigan State Press, 2018.
Hazony, Yoram. *God and Politics in Esther*. Cambridge, UK: Cambridge University Press, 2016.
Huleatt, Veery, ed. *The Two Ways: The Early Christian Vision of Discipleship from the Didache and the Shepherd of Hermas*. Translated by Michael W. Holmes. Walden, NY: Plough, 2018.
Hume, David. *An Enquiry Concerning the Principles of Morals*. Edited by J. B. Schneewind. Indianapolis: Hackett, 1983.
———. *Treatise of Human Nature*. Toronto: HarperTorch Classics, 2014.
Jerome. *Jerome: Letters and Selected Works*. Edited by Philip Schaff and Henry Wace. Translated by W. H. Fremantle. Nicene and Post-Nicene Fathers, 2nd ser., 6. Grand Rapids: Eerdmans, 1892.
Laistner, M. L. W. *Christianity and Pagan Culture in the Later Roman Empire*. Ithaca, NY: Cornell University Press, 1951.
Lewis, C. S. *The Abolition of Man*. New York: HarperOne, 2015. Kindle.
———. *An Experiment in Criticism*. Cambridge, UK: Cambridge University Press, 1961. Kindle.
———. *The Silver Chair*. New York: HarperCollins, 1953.
Liddell, Henry George, et al. *A Greek-English Lexicon*. Oxford, UK: Clarendon, 1968.
Lossky, Vladimir. *The Mystical Theology of the Eastern Church*. Crestwood, NY: St. Vladimir's Seminary Press, 1997.
Lukianoff, Greg, and Jonathan Haidt. *The Coddling of the American Mind: How Good Intentions and Bad Ideas Are Setting Up a Generation for Failure*. New York: Penguin, 2018.
MacIntyre, Alasdair. *After Virtue: A Study in Moral Theory*. Notre Dame, IN: Notre Dame University Press, 1981.
———. *Three Rival Versions of Moral Enquiry: Encyclopaedia, Genealogy, and Tradition*. Notre Dame, IN: University of Notre Dame Press, 1990.

———. *Whose Justice? Which Rationality?* Notre Dame, IN: University of Notre Dame, 1988.
Malone, Mary T. *The First Thousand Years*. Vol. 1 of *Women and Christianity*. Maryknoll, NY: Orbis, 2000.
Manson, Jamie. "Oprah and the Triumph of the Therapeutic." *National Catholic Reporter*, May 25, 2011. https://www.ncronline.org/blogs/grace-margins/oprah-and-triumph-therapeutic.
Marno, David. *Death Be Not Proud: The Art of Holy Attention*. Edited by Kathryn Lofton and John Lardes Modern. Chicago: University of Chicago Press, 2016.
Martyr, Justin. *Justin Martyr and Athenagoras*. Edited by Alexander Roberts and James Donaldson. Translated by Marcus Dods et al. Ante-Nicene Christian Library 2. Edinburgh: T&T Clark, 1870.
McCarthy, Margaret. "The Slavery of Radical Freedom." First Things, Aug. 21, 2020. https://www.firstthings.com/web-exclusives/2020/08/the-slavery-of-radical-freedom.
Meltzoff, Andrew N. "Out of the Mouths of Babes: Imitation, Gaze, and Intentions in Infant Research—The "Like Me" Framework." In *Mimesis and Science: Empirical Research on Imitation and the Mimetic Theory of Culture and Religion*, edited by Scott R. Garrels, 55–74. East Lansing: Michigan State University Press, 2011.
Moreschini, Claudio, and Enrico Norelli. *Early Christian Greek and Latin Literature: A Literary History*. Translated by Matthew J. O'Connell. Peabody, MA: Hendrickson, 2005.
Nazianzen, Gregory. *Funeral Orations by St. Gregory Nazianzen and St. Ambrose*. Edited by Roy J. Deferrari. Translated by Leo P. McCauley. Fathers of the Church 22. Washington, DC: Catholic University of America Press, 1953.
Nestle, Eberhard. *Bible: New Testament Greek Text with Critical Apparatus*. London: British and Foreign Bible Society, 1904.
O'Conner, Flannery. *Mystery and Manners*. New York: Farrar, Straus and Giroux, 1990.
Palmer, G. E. H., et al., eds. and trans. *The Philokalia: The Complete Text*. London: Faber and Faber, 1983.
Palmer, Richard E. *Hermeneutics: Interpretation Theory in Schleiermacher, Dilthey, Heidegger, and Gadamer*. Evanston, IL: Northwestern University Press, 1969.
Prior, Karen Swallow. "The Art of Virtuous Reading: In Our Digitized World, We Read More Than Ever. But We've Lost the Connection between Good Books and Good Character." *Christianity Today* 63, no. 1 (Jan. 2019) 34–38.
———. *On Reading Well: Finding the Good Life through Great Books*. Grand Rapids: Brazos, 2018.
Rieff, Philip. *The Triumph of the Therapeutic: Uses of Faith after Freud*. Wilmington, DE: ISI, 2006.
Robinette, Brian DuWayne. "Deceit, Desire, and the Desert: René Girard's Mimetic Theory in Conversation with Early Christian Monastic Practice." In *Violence, Transformation, and the Sacred*, edited by Margaret Pfeil and Tobias L. Winright, 130–43. Maryknoll, NY: Orbis, 2012.
Schmemann, Alexander. *For the Life of the World*. Yonkers, NY: St Vladimir's Seminary Press, 2018.
Schram, Glenn N. "The New Gnosticism: The Philosopher Eric Voegelin Finds an Old Christian Heresy To Be Very Much Alive." *Crisis Magazine*, July 11, 2013. https://

www.crisismagazine.com/1990/the-new-gnosticism-the-philosopher-eric-voegelin-finds-an-old-christian-heresy-to-be-very-much-alive.
Smith, Adam. *The Theory of Moral Sentiments*. London: Bohn, 1853.
Sozomen, et al. *The Ecclesiastical History of Sozomen: Comprising a History of the Church from A. D. 324 to A. D. 440*. London: Bohn, 1855. Internet Archive, Aug. 22, 2006. https://archive.org/details/theecclesiastica00sozouoft/page/362/mode/2up.
Steenberg, M. C. *The Beginnings of a Life of Prayer*. Platina, CA: St. Herman of Alaska Brotherhood, 2012.
Steinbeck, John. *East of Eden*. New York: Penguin, 1952.
Stroup, George W., ed. *Reformed Reader*. Vol. 2 of *A Sourcebook in Christian Theology*. Louisville: Westminster/John Knox, 1993.
Voeglin, Eric. *Modernity without Restraint*. Vol. 5 of *Collected Works of Eric Voegelin*. Edited by Manfred Henningsen. Columbia: University of Missouri Press, 2000.
Volz, Carl A. "Genius of Chrysostom's Preaching." *Christian History* 13, no. 4 (Jan. 1, 1994) 24–26.
Waters, John. "Books about Next to Nothing." First Things, Mar. 10, 2020. https://www.firstthings.com/web-exclusives/2020/03/books-about-next-to-nothing.
Weissbourd, Richard. *The Parents We Mean to Be: How Well-Intentioned Adults Undermine Children's Moral and Emotional Development*. Boston: Houghton Mifflin Harcourt, 2009.
Williams, Rowan. "The Embodied Logos: The Renewal of Mind and the Transformation of Sense." Keynote lecture given at Patterson Triennial Conference, Fordham University, NY, June 4, 2019.
Woodill, Joseph. *The Fellowship of Life: Virtue Ethics and Orthodox Christianity*. Washington, DC: Georgetown University Press, 1998.
Yannaras, Christos. *The Freedom of Morality*. Translated by Elizabeth Briere. Crestwood, NY: St. Vladimir's Seminary Press, 1996.
———. *The Meaning of Reality: Essays on Existence and Communion, Eros and History*. Edited by Fr. Gregory Edwards and Herman A. Middleton. Los Angeles: Sebastian and Indiktos, 2011.

Subject Index

Alighieri, Dante. *See* Dante Alighieri.
alms-giving, 4, 40, 76
anthropology, 14, 60, 85, 92–93, 98, 121
   theological, 6, 17, 19, 61–62, 82, 89–90, 146
apatheia, 16, 47, 49, 51, 67, 69–70, 74
apophaticism, 53–55
   as an attitude, 53–57, 64, 67
   defined, 53
askesis, vii, 4, 16–17, 20, 29, 36, 39–41, 44, 46–61, 63–67, 69–71, 77, 79, 98–99, 102, 132, 142, 145–47
   defined, 4
Athanasius, Saint, 4, 24, 26–27, 29, 31–32, 44, 90, 150
Augustine, Saint, 33, 91, 150
autexousion, 80, 85–86, 90, 92
   defined, 85

Bambi (Stalten), 104
baptism, 29, 60, 64, 66–67, 102, 140, 147
Basil of Caesarea, Saint, 4–5, 27, 29, 32, 56, 68
Bottum, Joseph, 21, 118–23, 142, 146, 150
   Decline of the Novel, The, 21, 118–19, 150

Christlikeness, 24, 28–29, 33, 35, 39, 42, 45, 48, 52, 61, 66, 69–70, 80, 84, 88, 106–07, 132, 142, 151

Christian life, 4–7, 22, 26–27, 34, 36, 42, 50, 60, 64–65, 106, 147
Christianity, 4–5, 17, 24, 26, 28, 32–33, 38, 44, 47, 51, 101, 111, 113, 116, 120, 125, 143–44, 147, 150, 152–54
   Eastern, 5–7, 16–17, 32, 36, 59, 62–63, 82
   as a tradition, 116–17
   Western, 5, 54
church, the, 3, 14, 23–24, 26–27, 31, 35, 37, 40, 42, 49–50, 56, 58, 61–65, 102–04, 112, 116–17, 126–27, 145, 154
   and eschatology, 61, 65
   sacramental life of, 27
   as *theandric*, 62, 117
Christlikeness. *See* Jesus Christ, likeness of.
Clement of Alexandria, Saint, 26, 29
   Christ the Educator, 26
conscience, 66, 86–88, 105–06, 126, 142
   as hub of moral life, 87, 106, 142
   as an inborn human capacity, 86–88
   as inner judge, 87
   as teacher, 87, 106
Constitutions of Holy Apostles, 25

Dante Alighieri, 69, 105
David, King, 72, 87, 102
Diadochos of Photiki, Saint, 75
Didache, 24–25, 152

SUBJECT INDEX

education, 1, 3, 7, 11, 13, 17, 28–29, 38–39, 52, 88, 105, 129, 142, 147
   classical, 7, 27, 111
   Christian, 5, 24, 26, 32–33, 42, 143
   early Christians on, 24–25
   moral, 3, 5, 11, 21, 23–24, 28, 46–48, 51–52, 62, 64, 65, 77, 79, 89, 92, 111, 116–17, 121, 127, 142–45, 147
egalitarianism, 12, 104, 133
emotivism, 2, 7, 8, 12–13, 128, 143–45
   defined, 8
Emulation. *See* Imitation.
Enlightenment, The, 2–3, 10, 13, 16, 112, 118–19, 143
Ephrem, Saint, 77, 151
Esther, Queen, 72–73, 151
Evagrius Ponticus, 16, 46–47, 68–70, 73, 80, 90, 93, 98–99, 153
   life of, 68
   psychology, 16, 68–69, 80, 93, 98–99
evil, 14–17, 38, 41, 52, 61, 72, 80, 82, 85, 88–89, 91–92, 97, 100, 106, 119, 140, 146, 150
   meonic, 90, 106
existentialism, 9–10, 18
   atheistic, 10
   Nietzschean, 7, 9, 143, 145
Exodus, The, 61, 147
Ezekiel, Prophet, 7

fall, the, 61, 71, 79, 82, 89–91, 98, 101
fasting, 4, 40, 55, 67, 69, 71–77
Felicitas, Saint, 104
Fletcher, Joseph, 9–10, 18, 84, 121, 151
Freedom, 4, 9–10, 18–19, 39, 46, 60, 84, 115, 133, 145, 150, 153
   autonomy, 14–15, 19–20, 59, 82, 90–91, 106, 126, 132, 145
   Christian, 15–16, 50, 56, 63, 67, 69–70, 75, 91, 133
   false, 14–15, 126
   moral, 80–85, 90, 96, 106
   from the passions, 39, 67–69, 91, 102, 133

Girard, René, vi, 6–7, 16, 19–21, 46, 93–96, 122, 125, 144, 146, 150–51, 153
   on *mimesis*, 93, 98–102, 105, 121
   on the novelistic conversion, 19, 121
   on novelistic knowledge, 121
gnosticism, 7, 12–14, 143, 145, 153–54
God, vi, 4, 10, 12, 17, 19, 24, 26–29, 33, 35–37, 39–41, 47–48, 52–61, 63–67, 69–88, 90–92, 98–103, 106, 109, 115, 117–118, 120, 129, 132–133, 136, 138, 141, 146–148, 150, 152
   alienation from, 15, 17, 86, 88, 106, 120, 132, 145
   ascent to, 54, 59, 70
   the Creator, 12, 14, 81, 84, 86, 136, 145
   energies of, 58
   the Father, vi, 15, 33–34, 56, 58, 63, 71, 99, 101, 103, 132–133
   fear of, 25, 56
   image of, 42, 80–81, 94, 98, 133
   kingdom of, 33, 35, 47, 58, 60, 65–67, 102, 104, 112, 138, 141, 148
   likeness of, 4, 15, 34, 52, 61, 64, 80, 83, 133
   as love, 84
Gregory the Great, Saint, 133
Gregory Nazianzen/us, Saint, 27, 55–56, 153, 155
Gregory of Nyssa, Saint, 4, 27, 29, 53, 63, 81, 152
Gregory of Sinai, Saint, 71, 74

Harakas, Stanley, 4, 17, 89, 152
Hauerwas, Stanley, 115
Holy Spirit, The, 4, 33–34, 41, 48, 62, 69, 71, 77, 88
   and the church, 61–62, 65, 102, 116
   cooperation with, 6, 36, 39, 48, 50, 63, 65, 67, 70, 84, 106
   and conversion, 40, 64–65
   grace, 52, 63–64, 67, 102
   at Pentecost, 62, 117
   temple of, 103

human, 3-4, 6, 8, 10-11, 14, 17-19, 23, 27, 59-62, 69-70, 78-81
  capacities, 10, 17, 19, 78-81, 88-90, 92-94, 100-101, 106-107, 146
  condition, 17-18, 80, 118-119
  kind, 56, 58, 61, 83, 86, 89-90, 93, 96, 145
  nature, 4, 6, 8, 17, 19, 23, 59-62, 78, 80-81, 83, 94, 106, 122, 124, 129, 152
  telos, 11, 14, 27, 59-61, 69-70, 80, 83-84
Hume, David, 8, 10, 121, 129, 152
hypostasis(es), 55-57, 82-83, 90-91, 106

imitation, vii, 16-17, 19, 21, 26, 41-44, 47-48, 57, 75, 78-80, 82, 84, 88-89, 92-93, 96, 99-107, 111, 117, 121, 125, 131, 142-43, 147, 151, 153. *See also mimesis*.

Jerome, Saint, 24, 28, 152
Jesus Christ, 7, 16, 26, 33, 47, 52, 59-62, 64, 81, 102, 147
  as the incarnation, 4, 6, 17, 26, 53, 58-60, 62, 146, 150
  likeness of, 24, 28-29, 33-35, 39-40, 42, 45, 48, 52, 54, 61, 64, 66, 69-70, 79-80, 84, 88, 106-07, 132, 142, 151
  as the pedagogue, 26
  and salvation, 26-27, 35, 52, 59-61, 113
  as the second Adam, 50, 59, 79
  as the Second Person of the Trinity, 59-61, 82
  as the real/true human, 52, 81, 106
John Cassian, Saint, 46-47, 73-74, 82
John Climacus, 37

koinonia, 82-83

Lewis, C.S., 15, 21, 108, 127-31, 133-34, 136-37, 139-42, 146, 152
  Abolition of Man, The, 128-30, 142, 152
  "An Experiment in Criticism," 127-28, 131, 152
  on the literary person, 128
  Silver Chair, The, 21, 108, 135-37, 139-41, 146
  on the *Tao*, 15, 129
Lossky, Vladimir, 17, 53-59, 62-64, 81, 83-84, 116-17, 146, 152

MacIntyre, Alasdair, 2-3, 6, 20, 108, 111, 128, 141, 143-44, 146, 152
  After Virtue, 2, 6-8, 20-21, 111, 114, 116, 128, 152
  on the narratable life, 6, 20-21
Makarios of Egypt, Saint, 71, 74
Mary (Virgin), 103
Mary of Bethany, Saint, 103-04
Mary Magdalene, Saint, 69, 103-04
marriage, 5, 15, 23, 28, 30, 33-36, 150
  purpose of, 33
Maximus the Confessor, Saint, 4, 16-17, 59, 62, 70-71, 75-76, 84, 90-92
McCarthy, Margaret, 14-15, 153
mentorship, 80, 102, 104-05, 126, 142, 153
mimesis, 16, 19-20, 41, 43, 46-48, 50, 78, 84, 92-94, 96, 98, 101-03, 105-06, 107, 121-22, 142, 146, 150-51, 153
  acquisitive, 46, 94, 102, 106
  positive, 19-20, 41, 46-48, 92, 98, 101-03, 107, 142, 146
  See also, imitation.
mimetic theory, 6, 19, 46, 80, 92-93, 96, 101, 122, 146, 151, 153
mimetic crisis, 99
mimetic rivalry, 94-00, 106
models, 15, 23, 42, 47, 105-06,
morality, 2-5, 7-9, 11-13, 15-16, 18, 22, 49, 78-80, 82-85, 90-92, 96, 106, 112, 115, 126, 130, 141, 143-45, 151-52, 154
  capacities for, 78-80
  Freedom of. *See* Freedom, moral.
  moral apocalypse, 24
  moral formation, 1, 23, 41, 49, 52, 92, 105, 108, 123, 142, 144, 146
  moral imagination, 21, 124, 129-30, 152
  of tradition, 2, 5, 143-45

Moses, Prophet, 27, 54, 56, 61, 102, 136, 141, 147, 148, 152

narrative, 20, 37, 44, 72–73, 81, 100, 109, 117, 122, 146
natural law, 27, 88–89, 106
Nietzsche, Friedrich, 10, 12, 18–19, 101, 113, 121

obedience, 21, 34, 64, 101, 103, 108, 132–33, 136, 138–40, 146–47

parable, 35, 65, 105
parenthood, 1, 15, 33–37, 39, 152
   aim of, 33–36, 39
passions, the, 4, 8, 36, 39, 48–51, 60, 67–70, 75, 77–78, 80, 91–92, 99, 102, 106, 109–10, 132–33
   bodily, 60, 68–69, 75, 106
   defined, 39
   freedom from, 39, 67–69, 91, 133
   of the soul, 69, 106
Paul, Saint, 24, 33, 36–37, 41–42, 74, 87, 102–03
Perpetua, Saint, 104
personhood, 56, 81–85, 88, 107
Peter of Damascus, Saint, 76
Philokalia, 16–17, 70–71, 73–77, 132, 146, 153
Pinocchio (Collodi), 52, 151
post-Enlightenment, 5–7, 12–14, 16, 18–20, 52, 144–45
Prager, Dennis, 1
prayer, 4, 36–37, 40, 47, 67, 70–73, 75–77, 99, 125, 135, 142, 151, 154
Prior, Karen Swallow, 21, 122–25, 127–28, 130, 142, 146, 153
prosopon, 82

Rieff, Philip, 7, 11–12, 153

sanctification, 33, 36, 39, 51–52, 54, 60–61, 66, 92, 118, 120, 129
sarx (flesh), 60,
Schleiermacher, Friedrich, 10, 153
sin, 9, 14, 17, 30, 37, 39, 41, 59–61, 69, 78–80, 82, 89–92, 97, 99–00, 106, 132, 140, 146, 150

Smith, Adam, 12, 154
soma (body), 60, 74
spiritual exercise. See *askesis*.
spiritual formation, vii, 4–5, 7, 16–17, 20, 25, 29, 33, 35, 49–52, 54, 62–63, 78–79, 108, 126, 128, 144, 146
Steinbeck, John, 15, 82, 96–97, 154
Stephen, Saint, 96, 104
story-telling, vii, 17, 19–21, 23, 43–45, 48–50, 107–147
   to affirm truth, 118
   through drama, 45, 109
subjectivism, 7–9, 143, 145

Tao. See Lewis, C.S. on the *Tao*.
theosis, 19–20, 51–52, 61, 63–64
   defined, 63
therapeutic movement, the, 7, 11–12, 145
tradition, 2–3, 5–7, 11, 13, 16–17, 20–21, 24, 26, 29, 33, 36, 47, 63, 82, 103, 108, 111–21, 127–29, 141–47, 151–52
   alternatives to, 7–13, 112–13, 121, 143
   as community, 11, 21, 115–16, 146
   defined, 112, 117
   as history, 114–15
   as story-formed/shaped, 115, 127
   as *techne*, 114
Trinity, the, 17, 53, 55–62, 78, 82, 146
   unity of, 57, 62

vainglory, 16, 23, 32–33, 36–41, 44–45, 48–50, 71, 74–75, 77, 79, 99, 109–10, 125, 131, 143–44, 150
   defined, 37
virtue, 4, 7–9, 16–17, 20–21, 26–27, 30, 35–40, 42, 44, 48–49, 54, 57, 63, 68–70, 73, 75, 77, 79, 90, 98, 101–02, 107–08, 114–15, 119, 123–27, 131–33, 136, 142, 146, 152, 154
   cultivation of, 16, 21, 26, 36, 48, 73, 107, 115, 124–25, 142
   true, 27

vicarious practice of, 21, 48, 123–27, 142
Voegelin, Eric, 12, 153–54

Weissbourd, Richard, 11–12, 154

Yannaras, Christos, 18–19, 56–57, 82–84, 90–92, 115, 154